M000311704

FOR THE

Love OF A

Child

MY LIFE, MY CITY & MY MISSION

HARVEY WEISENBERG

SQUAREONE
PUBLISHERS

COVER DESIGNER: Jeannie Tudor
EDITOR: Liza Burby
TYPESETTER: Gary A. Rosenberg

Square One Publishers
115 Herricks Road
Garden City Park, NY 11040
(516) 535-2010 • (877) 900-BOOK
www.squareonepublishers.com

Library of Congress Cataloging-in-Publication Data
Names: Weisenberg, Harvey, 1933- author.
Title: For the love of a child / Harvey Weisenberg.
Description: Garden City Park, NY : Square One Publishers, [2019] | Includes

  bibliographical references and index.
Identifiers: LCCN 2018044127 (print) | LCCN 2018045714 (ebook) | ISBN
  9780757054808 (e-book) | ISBN 9780757004803 (pbk. : alk. paper)
Subjects: LCSH: Weisenberg, Harvey, 1933- | Cerebral palsy—Biography. |
  People with disabilities—Biography. | Father and son—Biography.
Classification: LCC RC388 (ebook) | LCC RC388 .W45 2019 (print) | DDC
  616.8/360092 [B] —dc23
LC record available at https://lccn.loc.gov/2018044127

ISBN-13: Print: 978-0-7570-0480-3; Ebook: 978-0-7570-5480-8

Printed in the United States of America

10   9   8   7   6   5   4   3   2

Contents

To Ellen Weisenberg

Her love and empathy for our community and its people,
especially for those with special needs,
will remain her legacy.
Her beauty and elegance will blossom every spring
in her garden nestled next to the Long Beach boardwalk
and shall live on in our hearts.

Acknowledgments

A heartfelt thanks to the many members and staff of the New York State Assembly and Senate who I worked with during my 25 years in Albany, especially the Senate Majority leaders and the Assembly speakers. We served during a time when many people lost faith in government. These are not times for the faint of heart. So, here's to all the true public servants, both past and present, who stayed the course, and kept fighting for the underserved, the forgotten, and the disenfranchised. In the end, these are things that matter.

A special thank you to Governors Cuomo, Pataki, Spitzer, Paterson, and Cuomo, and their staff, especially the ones who weren't entirely successful at avoiding me when I got persistent. We built beautiful things together and made life better for people who needed us. That's what gets us out of bed every day and I hope all of you will continue fighting the good fight.

To the NYS Legislative Messenger Service, the finest and most efficient group of people in Albany. You lifted me up every day. You reminded me, in so many ways you'll never know, of why I came to Albany in the first place. All of you were like a beam of sunshine that never failed to make my day. You will always have a place in my heart.

I was so fortunate to have many good people with me through the years. My very dear friend Tom DiNapoli and I have been together through everything over the years. Jerry Kremer gave me the chance to run for his Assembly seat. David Mack, a friend for over sixty years, who worked tirelessly behind the scenes to help so many others in their times of need. Mike Roseingrave, who ran my constituent services in the Long Beach office, was with me from the first day I took office, until the last day of my last term. Mike gave his life to serving my constituents and he will always have my respect and regard. Marie Curley, my Albany Chief of Staff, is a seasoned political insider who never hesitated to tell me the hard truths.

A huge thank you to my dear friends Walter Belling and Jerry Fleischman. They ensured my campaign accounts were kept in order, and helped me get elected and re-elected to both local and state offices. Also Bobby Smith, Stanley Fleishman, Larry Elovich, Donna Romang Caldera, Ellen Rosen, and Steve Kohut. These individuals were my political allies and genuine comrades who were always at my side.

A special thank you to Liza N. Burby for her help in putting this book together. It couldn't have been done without her. I also thank Rudy Shur and his staff at Square One Publishers for bringing this book to light.

And last, but certainly not least, I want to thank my wife Ellen, who was and since is my inspiration, and my children Vicki, Russell (and his wife Marilyn), Julie (and her husband Donald), and Gregg (and his wife Sogdianna)—and to my six grandchildren, Michael, Danny, Jackie, Brock, Max and Zac. It is never easy to spend time away from your family fighting for others. It is a sacrifice that I knowingly chose to bear. I hope they know that they have always been in my heart and in my thoughts—even if I hadn't expressed it enough. And to my sister Brenda and her husband Howard Siegal, who have always been there for me.

Introduction

Even though I retired from the New York State Assembly in 2014, there isn't a week that goes by that I don't receive a call from someone looking for my help and advice concerning their special needs child. They tell me tragic stories about their sons and daughters who have been suspended from public and private schools for poor behavior, when in reality they should have received services for their special need. Others have a child whose behavior issues make placement in a needs program difficult for them. Parents call to ask how they can get better care for their institutionalized child who is already totally dependent on their caregivers for food and other basic needs, and has to wait until someone has extra time to give them a hug or hold them. I hear from family members who have someone who has aged out of the programs they've been entitled to, and they need help with next steps. Independent living housing is another frequent topic, because in our system there's a waiting list of twelve thousand or more for special needs adults who can no longer live at home with their families.

These parents contact me because they know I have been fighting for the needs of our most vulnerable citizens—people with severe physical and mental disabilities—for over thirty-eight years. They are aware that I know from experience that for every appalling story I hear, there are solutions to fight for. Among these is teaching all able-bodied individuals who are in the position to make a difference for special needs people—the teachers, medical professionals, and politicians—that these people have value to our society, and they need us to advocate for them. They may also know that I learned from my son Ricky and his mother, my wife of forty-eight years, Ellen, that special needs children have so

1

much unconditional love to give the rest of us. It is my mission to make sure that everyone else learns that too.

I have been a ferocious champion for people with special needs, which has mattered to me since I first met my Ellen and saw the love she had to give to her child Ricky. In fact, her love and devotion to her child, who was born with cerebral palsy and was unable to speak or cry, was what most attracted me to her at first—though it didn't go unnoticed by me that she was also extremely beautiful and kind. I think I was very brave to approach her that day in 1965 at the Coral Reef Beach Club in Long Beach where I was working as a lifeguard, because I was intimidated by her beauty, as well as her life experience and knowledge.

I quickly realized what a gift it would be to go through life with such a wonderful and caring person as my partner, to have her in my life for my own two boys, and to enlighten me about all that I still needed to learn. We had a love that is everlasting and I believe God set this up for us. We celebrated fifty years of total happiness before she passed away on April 18, 2016, and I miss her every minute of every day. This account is in part about Ellen and the relationship we were blessed with. In the book, I'll talk more about meeting Ellen. Our partnership encompassed the rest of the stories told in this book as well, as she was present for all my work for the City of Long Beach, and my work on behalf of the state, usually attending meetings by my side.

This is also a story about my oldest son Ricky. I watched Ellen's early struggles to care for him. When she could no longer do so on her own, in part because she also had two little girls at home and was dealing with her own health issues, she found him a group home for children with intellectual disabilities where she hoped he would thrive. A few short weeks later she discovered with horror that her child had suffered physically and emotionally at the hands of his paid caregivers at this state-supported institution, Wassaic State School in upstate New York. This experience was the beginning of Ellen's and my own awareness of the complex and horrifying inadequacies of services available for children with special needs.

Everyone who ever met Ellen loved her because she always had a smile. She never had anything except a kind word to say about anybody. That is the way Ricky still is, even though he was mistreated in not just that first, but also a second group home, Allegheny School in Pittsburgh, Pennsylvania, before we could rescue him—and then again when he was in his fifties. Yet these experiences never changed his personality of being sweet and good. He is now a sixty-year-old man and he has never caused any trouble to anybody. We still get birthday cards and mail from his direct care workers from twenty years ago who remember Ricky as the person he is, and that's a reflection of who Ellen was as well. There's more to tell about Ricky's story, so a section of the book will focus on my special son.

I also want to share stories about the people who inspired me early on, including my big family of parents and my sister, my grandparents, aunts, uncles, and cousins, almost all of whom called Long Beach home. I was brought up surrounded by a loving family who taught me these values: to be healthy, to be fair, and to give happiness to others. Their love and closeness moved me to want to care for others early in my life, so I started my career as a police officer long before entering politics. (There will be more on my varied career, which for most of my life included two jobs at once.)

I have also been motivated by the city I have lived in for all but my first year of life. My history as a resident of Long Beach has impacted my public service activities in profound ways. That is why in Chapter One I include not only the stories of my family members who influenced me and the coaches who inspired me, but also my early history with this special barrier island off the South Shore of Long Island.

I believe that God gave me an angel in Ricky, a saint in Ellen, and thanks to both of them, a mission to spend the rest of my life making sure that Ricky and children like him won't suffer. Throughout this book, I'll share the work I did and why it mattered, as well as the people Ellen and I met, and the experiences we had along the way. Though the work will never be completely done, during my career I have had a hand in passing ground-breaking legislation and programs that have made a difference in the lives of special needs children and the people who love and care for them.

But I didn't just work on issues regarding people with disabilities. I have also pushed through other laws to crack down on drunken driving and sexual predators; increase transparency in government; and increase funding for police, firefighters, and other first responders. I even found a way at age sixty-nine, posing in my Speedo on a billboard, to draw attention to the need for sun protection when I became concerned about the lack of expiration dates on sunblock lotions. To this

day people talk to me about that billboard. For years it was a landmark
that people would use to give directions. They'd say things like, "I'm
here with Harvey at Rockaway Turnpike." There were also countless
laws to protect the environment, particularly for my beloved Long
Beach. In all, I got three-hundred and thirty-seven bills signed into law
during my time in office. Some issues may seem narrow, but many have
national resonance and provide valuable political lessons in how to get
things done.

At the same time, I believe all politicians are only as good as the
citizens they represent, and I am no exception. I have been blessed to
work with countless citizen heroes who have inspired me time and
time again. Many were parents who suffered tremendous adversity,
but came back fighting to make sure that others wouldn't go through
the same agony. Their tragic losses led to important legislation like
Leandra's Law, which imposes tough penalties on adults who drive
drunk with children in the car; the passage of Louis's Law, which made
it a requirement that all public schools have life-saving defibrillators
(AEDs); and Jonathan's Law, which entitles parents and legal guardians
access to all child abuse investigation files and medical history records.

Still other heroes were volunteers at community centers, police
officers, fire fighters, social workers, and consumer advocates. When
Superstorm Sandy hit New York and New Jersey, I saw armies of volunteers from here and around the country. They muscled through the
wet, the cold, and the chaos to provide shelter and relief to thousands
of people who had lost their homes. These are good people who force
politicians to be good, and they make a difference. In the book I focus on
all the issues I fought for, both the causes I found on my own, and the
ones brought to my attention by people who needed my help to muscle
them onto the table of our State government.

As a Democrat, I was an elected official for thirty-eight years, thirteen
as a council member for the City of Long Beach and twenty-five in Albany.
Throughout my time in politics I was able to work in a bipartisan way.
I have worked—and in some cases wrestled with—New York leaders,
like Mario Cuomo, George Pataki, David Paterson, Eliot Spitzer, Chuck
Schumer, and Hillary Clinton. I have come under fire from both liberals
and conservatives. I've been conservative on issues like law enforcement
and reverence for the American flag, but I've also been a staunch supporter of gay marriage, abortion rights, and religious tolerance.

I am one of the happiest people I know. I didn't always win. I got into fights within my own party's leadership—still do—and I've been double-crossed more than once. Governor Mario Cuomo once called me tenacious, but he didn't mean it as a compliment. I had forced his hand on a bill, and he was irritated with me. I've scraped with every governor since then as well—George Pataki, Eliot Spitzer, David Paterson, and Andrew Cuomo. But I never stopped trying, and I'm glad I didn't.

As a matter of fact, because of the message I sent about politics—that as a legislator my priorities were not for political parties, but for the people—my colleagues respected that. Therefore, most of my legislation passed with unanimous consent by both Democrats and Republicans. I even have a resolution signed by every Democrat and Republican from Long Island thanking me for my years of service.

I can also say that I am still impacting the families, agencies, and schools with my knowledge, information, and experience about why it's so important to have trained professionals to be able to help the people who are the neediest. The most discriminated people in our society are those with disabilities, and unfortunately it's the most difficult job in the world to take care of another person. Anyone who has that chore understands that there are people in government making monetary decisions that don't make this their top priority. I'm still making politicians aware that it has to be their main concern. The health and safety of human beings and the treatment, dignity, and respect that they're entitled to are not present if you are understaffed, overworked, and underpaid. When that happens, you have consequences like the ones you'll learn about in this book.

Anyone who knows me is aware that I have never had any trouble speaking my mind. I have been called blunt more than once. I have given hundreds of speeches, but I have never written one down in my life. That's because God gave me this ability to speak out and express my feelings. I always speak with my mind and heart about the things that matter most to me. Recently I spoke at Hofstra University in Uniondale, New York, where I received an honorary doctorate degree. I explained to the parents and students there that for me success is defined as being happy with what you do, not how many financial rewards you receive and how many dollars you make. That's why I chose public service, because the biggest reward I could possibly get comes from the heart-felt "thank yous" I still receive on a daily basis.

Even these days, when I take my daily walk on the boardwalk, eight out of ten people come to say thank you to me, some I don't even know. The work I have done with Ellen touched thousands of peoples' lives all over this country. We had the experience of being able to help families with special needs give their family members quality of life in a safe environment. I have dedicated my life to insuring the removal of barriers, improving access, and enhancing the quality of life for those who are challenged. To me, that is one of the things that has made my life rewarding.

This is the story of my life, but it is also a story about the resilience of people with disabilities and their families—and those who fight to make a difference in their lives. Above all, it is a love story as I define it to make the world understand that we can all learn from special children what unconditional love means. It's also a love story about my life with Ellen, and how important it is to have happiness. It is a story that is important to me that I share with you, so thank you for taking this journey with me.

I.

The People and Place
That Inspired Me

have been lucky to be a part of a family who has had so much love
and caring for each other, which you so rarely see nowadays. Everybody in my family has only brought happiness and joy to the world. I
am so grateful for that.

Though I was born in the Bronx on December 31, 1933, less than
a year later my parents, grandparents, and all but one aunt moved to
Long Beach, Long Island where I have lived ever since. My mother,
Renee Scheckwitz, had three younger sisters and a brother, and all were
part of the Long Beach family that surrounded me throughout my childhood. My sister Brenda and I can't remember which one of them moved
out here first, but we do know that once one did, they all followed.

My parents and I moved into the Broadway Apartments at 25 West
Broadway overlooking the Atlantic Ocean. My grandparents, Grandma
Kate and Grandpa Louie Scheckwitz, who was a furrier, lived in the
building too, and so did Uncle Al and his family. Aunt Millie and her
family lived just two blocks away on East Chester Street, and Aunt Maxine was on Hudson Street. My mother's other sister, Aunt Gladys, was
the only one who didn't live nearby. She and Uncle Nathan "Lippy"
lived in Brooklyn, but she came out every weekend for our family meals.

My father, Harry Weisenberg, at two-hundred and thirty pounds
and six feet tall, was known by his peers as Big Harry. He worked in a
defense plant on Long Island during World War II, and was admired
for his generosity and his strength. He once won a contest for carrying
the most steel at work. He was also athletic, often playing softball on

National Boulevard. His three brothers, my Uncles Ben, Max, and Frank, were originally in the coal business in New York City. They would come out from the Bronx to Long Beach to spend time with my family, and we would go into the city to see them. What I remember best about them is that they'd give me shiny new pennies.

My parents, aunts, and uncles weren't the only family I was lucky to enjoy spending time with. I also had many cousins. The boys were born first: Dickie, then Saul, then me, and Donnie. We were all very close. It's worth mentioning, since I am such a large man, that I was born premature at only four pounds and had to be in an incubator. My mother had four miscarriages before me.

Then the girls were born, including my sister Brenda, and cousins Carol, Margie, Susan, and then later Iris and Paul. We were brothers and sisters with everyone. Saul, Susan, and Paul grew up in Brooklyn. But the rest of us children played together; they were just a part of my life growing up. We also went through the school system together from kindergarten through high school. Everyone knew everyone and cared about each other. It was an unbelievable way to grow up.

We also ate together as a family and extended family on every occasion. Every Sunday all eighteen of us—my grandparents, parents, aunts, uncles, and cousins—would have brunch together in our grandparents' studio apartment. It only had a Pullman kitchen, which had a sink, stove, and refrigerator all on one wall. Yet somehow enough food was prepared for all of us. Our Seders were always experienced in our grandparents' place as well. But everybody also loved to come to our apartment because my mother loved to cook—her apple pie was a favorite of everyone's. And though like my grandmother she kept a kosher home, she did make bacon for her only son.

I remember each family gathering was always a festive and loving environment. The food was plentiful and the company superb. My cousins and I sat at the "children's table" long after we were kids because we were a big family, and where else were we going to sit? It was a blessing to have an environment with so much love spanning multiple generations: parents, grandparents, aunts, uncles, and cousins, and all of it centered around my beloved city, Long Beach.

Entertainment was also part of our gatherings. My aunts Maxine and Gladys had been the Lewis Sisters of Vaudeville in the 1920s. During World War II, Aunt Maxine sang, danced, and read dramatic poems in the theaters in the city to raise money for war bonds. She even once had top billing over Milton Berle. My aunts' penchant for performing was passed down to my sister Brenda and cousins Carol and Margie. During the polio epidemic in the 1940s, through my mother's influence, they created an annual show each August. They called it a "polio show" to raise money to support the March of Dimes. They would dance and sing out on the patio by the beach, and passersby would toss money into a box they set up. They once raised $ 86, which was quite a good box office rate for back then.

We all learned to dance and music was a part of our lives too. Uncle Sol, Aunt Maxine's husband, played the ukulele, and he taught Carol, Donnie, and Iris how to play. My mother played the piano and was skilled at classical music. Uncle Al performed in countless theater groups in Long Beach. He even appeared much later in an episode of the television show *The O.C.* Even though he only uttered one word, "Feh," he received a residual check for that appearance. Carrying on the performance gene these days is my nephew Kenny Siegel, Brenda's son, a songwriter, multi-instrumentalist, and music producer.

Being there for each other was just what we did, like the time there was a fire in the Broadway Apartments where we lived. That day I was walking home from a friend's house and saw that our six-story building was on fire. We all had to move out—my grandparents, Uncle Al's family, and us. We stayed with Aunt Millie and then moved into the Breakers Apartment on the boardwalk until we could go back.

While I'm sure the whole situation was upsetting for my parents and grandparents, in my memory there are two funny stories that stand out. When the fire started, my mother had been making a turkey dinner, which of course she had to leave behind. When we were allowed back in to get our belongings, we saw that our apartment had suffered water damage. We also discovered that all the food had been eaten by the firemen. Also, we had to wrap our valuables into sheets and drop them out the window. I remember my father put a bottle of scotch in with Brenda's things, and when it was tossed from the window, it broke all over them.

My Earliest Family Values

My entire family was also involved in the Long Beach community. All the men and boys played sports, like softball. My grandfather Louie liked to box on the beach in competitions and throw around a medicine ball. All of my family was also actively involved in community affairs. For instance, Aunt Millie was president of B'nai B'rith, and we helped her out with events. I was brought up with the lesson that if something is wrong there are two things you can do: avoid it or do something about it. My family always chose the latter—and I still do to this day.

My mother is among those people who stand out to me as someone who nurtured my need to make a difference with my life. She was a natural born caretaker, a social worker before there was even a title for it. My friends, my sister's friends, and anybody else who had a problem, went to my mother and always got advice and guidance in a positive way. She also fed any child who needed it, to the point that when I was small and more interested in playing than eating, she had to try to shove food in my mouth while I ran past her. I was the only child she was feeding who wasn't eating.

When Brenda wanted to join a Brownie troop, they wouldn't take her unless our mother became a leader. And so Mom did, taking the girls on camping trips and skating. Brenda recalls our mother felt sorry for the girl who couldn't skate, and when she tried to help her, Mom got pulled down on the ice. Our mother literally threw herself into that volunteer task, which was only one of many she devoted her life to. To this day, Brenda's friends still say our mother was the best scout leader.

It's no surprise that Brenda followed in our mother's footsteps. In Brenda's sixth grade autograph book there was a question, "What do you want to be?" She asked our mother what she should be when she grows up, and our mother answered "a social worker." When Brenda asked Mom what they do, she was told, "They care for people." Not only did Brenda become a social worker, she was also named a woman of distinction for the state of New York for her work. She spent more time working as a volunteer than she did working full-time helping others, including providing support to prisoners and to school children.

My sister, Brenda Siegel, is an amazing person even today, just like our mother was. When she was in high school, she was the head majorette and used to go into the elementary schools to teach kids how to twirl. She was still a young student, but she already had an interest in helping others. When she attended Ithaca College, she was head majorette there as well. Once they were competing against Long Beach, and she was so excited, she led the team to the parking lot instead of the field.

Later she married our Long Beach Good Humor man, Howie Siegel. In those days, they pedaled bicycle carts. Howie is also to be admired. He has old-fashioned values. He has never missed a day of work in sixty years, and he's always there to help Brenda and his extended family. This year he turns eighty.

Another person who was one of my heroes was Aunt Millie's husband, Maurice Fleischman, who we called Uncle Buster. He was a lawyer who became the Long Beach City Manager on January 1, 1950. The City Manager's job was to run the day-to-day operations of the city and its government, including the employees and the operating budget, and it paid $8,000 at the time. Prior to that, starting in 1944, he had served as city treasurer, corporation council, and acting City Manager. He was the City Manager until 1963, when he was asked to serve as the Deputy Comptroller of New York State under Arthur Levitt, Sr.

Uncle Buster was an influence because he took care of the city we all loved. My cousin, Marge, Uncle Buster's daughter, recalled that he loved everything about Long Beach. For him, the beaches had to be spotless. When he decided he didn't like the machines that strained the sand to keep it clean, he went to the factory to have them make a better machine. He got the Long Beach ice rink a Zamboni. He improved the water and sewage treatment plant. He also developed the Recreation Center located on Magnolia Boulevard on the Bay, which played an important part in my personal life and career. The commissioner for recreation then was Yale Newman and his assistant was James McCabe, who was also my freshman basketball coach. They both impacted the lives of many in a positive way, and they were loved by all.

Uncle Buster, who had played football at the University of Michigan, was also a frequent supporter of my athletic development. He drove up to see me run the State Championship at West Point, and after my victory there, he spoke to reporters of me participating in the 1956 Olympics. He was proud of me and made sure I knew it.

My Long Beach

My other inspiration has been the place I have always called home, my City by the Sea. At three miles long and half a mile wide, Long Beach is an island between the Atlantic Ocean and Reynolds Channel in Nassau County. The Atlantic is to the south and Lido Beach and Point Lookout to the east. Our white sand beach is 3.3 miles long with an adjacent boardwalk that's 2.2 miles long. This beach and boardwalk were as much a part of my childhood as my family.

When my family arrived in 1934, Orphan's Day was already an annual event each August during which a diverse group of boys and girls arrived from Brooklyn. This all-day event was an exciting one as the children were treated to ice cream, soda, and hot dogs while they spent the day swimming and playing on the beach. My family was among the many who volunteered to help serve food to them on the beach. I don't remember a lot about the experience other than that around that time, thinking I was funny, I told my sister, "If you're not good, I'm going to put you on the bus with those kids." Since she's seven years younger than me, it probably wasn't my finest big brother moment.

But what I said paled in comparison to what a boy told my mother that same summer. She was volunteering by delivering food to the children at tables. He told her, "I don't want any of that Jew food." It really shook my mother up. Considering that this was during the time of Hitler's rise to power in Germany, it was a terrible thing for my mother to have to hear when she was just trying to help give the kids a good experience.

During World War II, the Lido Hotel in Lido Beach was turned into a Naval base with five thousand Navy men, and the Masonic Temple on National Boulevard became a USO (United Service Organization). My mother worked as a secretary at the Naval base at the end of the war, while my father worked at the defense factory. Uncle Al was a bombardier in the Air Force. He was decorated with the Air Medal Oak Leaf Cluster and other citations for his many missions in Europe.

When the military people came into the railroad station to get to Lido, my friends and I would meet the trains. The soldiers would throw coins to us. I remember we had air raid drills with lights out and shades down. In fact, my friends and I used to volunteer to walk the streets to hand out flyers for how to prepare for the drills. The armed forces, preparing to take on any type of invasion, built a look-out tower by the boardwalk on Riverside Boulevard. When they stopped using it, my friends and I would go in and we'd look out at the ocean.

I also remember from that time—and it's still true today—that every religious group worked together to help each other, whether it was to rebuild when a religious home was damaged or to support each other in city-related issues. We had Temple Israel, Temple Beth-El, St. Ignatius Martyr, St. Mary of the Isle, and the People's Church. I remember Father Graham at St. Mary's and Father John Cass at St. Ignatius were religious leaders who participated in local government, and they worked with the Protestant People's Church, as well as with Reverend Jesse James Evans, pastor at the Christian Light Missionary Baptist Church. When the Christian Light Church burned down in 1962, the majority of our community, mostly white people, got together to help rebuild it. When Long Beach Regional Catholic School was being built by St. Mary's and St. Ignatius in 1953, many of that project's supporters were Jewish. We all functioned as one community. No one had to lock their doors or worry about their kids because we were all being watched by neighbors.

My Early Days as an Athlete

I don't think I fully appreciated the significance of that community during my childhood, because like a typical child, I was most interested in my own activities. These revolved around sports. I spent a lot of time running on the boardwalk—which I still do daily. There was a basket on the street and I used to shoot baskets from sunup to sundown, long before I got to high school, playing with guys who were a lot older. This gave me the experience to be successful in organized sports. My sports heroes started with the Vets, who played at St. Mary's. I used to go to their high school baseball and basketball games; I admired the guys who were playing varsity. My gym teachers also really mattered to me during every grade I attended in school. I once invited my elementary school physical education teacher to lunch at my house.

When I got to Long Beach High School, I played football, basketball, and ran track. I would have participated in baseball and soccer if the school didn't have a rule limiting students to three varsity sports. Basketball and wrestling were the same season or I would have joined the wrestling team too. In physical education class I once had to wrestle the future boxing champ Anthony Patti, and I thought he was going to kill me. Instead, I beat him. So I could have more experience with wrestling, I went to wrestling camp with my friend Billy Muirhead. Sadly, he died just a few years later, in 1953, when he fought in Korea.

We had a small student population at Long Beach High, and everyone played two sports. Because I was involved in three sports—basketball, football, and track—I was a young athlete who got a lot of attention. A "New York Post" article dated December 26, 1951 (though they misspelled my last name), said that I was a "lad with problems—the kind of problems all would like to have." That I couldn't make up my mind if I wanted to be "a track, basketball, or football star." I was one-hundred-seventy-five pounds and six-foot, two inches. I spent four years on the basketball court, where one newspaper called me the "rangy forward." The year 1950 to 1951 was a championship year for our team, the Marines, and I played the 1951 to 1952 season until I graduated that February.

My basketball coach and hero was Bobby Gersten, who graduated from North Carolina where he was a great all-around athlete. The guys I played with were great players who all went to college on basketball scholarships. Wendell McPhee went to Cornell; Rollin Perry, Harry Sacks, and Eddie Condon went to Harvard; I was at Niagara; Donald Walters was at Colgate, and Billy Shelley and Tom DeLuca were at New York University. Charlie Sorenson became a Rockville Centre police officer. When I was in college I'd play against some of them. Then I played in an adult recreation league and I beat out Eddie Hoffman who was All-American at the Merchant Marine Academy. These are the guys that I admired and respected, and they made me focus on what was important in my life.

When it came to track, I was a high school junior for my first year of participation. I was introduced to track through a local Jewish organization. I jumped the high-jump the old-fashioned way: just ran and jumped over the bar. Today they do gymnastics. The highest I jumped was five-seven, but now they're jumping over six feet.

In one month in 1951, I won the South Shore Championship, then the Nassau County Championship, then went on to win the Long Island 440 Yard Championship. This was followed by the New York State Championship at West Point, the competition that Uncle Buster came to see. I won first place that June day in 1951, capturing the quarter-mile and becoming the first Long Beach student ever to win that title in the state championship. Uncle Buster, as City Manager, presented me with an award after this win on behalf of the Long Beach Booster Club during their annual dinner.

Our sports were big news to our city, attracting the attention of our local press—which wasn't always a good thing. In a newspaper column by Cy Newman, during football season in fall 1951, he wrote that I was "using poor judgment in playing football." He said I had promise of "developing into one of the finest quarter-milers in the East and possibly in the country" because I had annexed the championships earlier in the year. During the first week of football practice I had broken a small bone in my foot, so was sidelined. I took the cast off myself so I could play the last two games of the season. I remember what my leg looked like when I did that; it had atrophied. I started to run and build it back up again just so I could get back to play. Maybe Cy Newman was right; I was taking quite a chance if track was the direction I was heading in.

But I was still a seventeen-year-old kid. There was a regular column Mr. GO (General Organization) in the local paper then in which they'd interview a "Popular Boy of the Month." The article said that I worked at the Long Beach Miniature Golf Course during the summer and that I like popular music. My favorite song at the time, according to the article, was King Cole's rendition of "Too Young." And my mother's apple pie was my favorite dessert. It was all true. But I also worked at Waller's Ice Cream store, and I toasted rolls at the Hebrew National store. Those shops and the golf course were along the boardwalk. I asked to get paid in singles and I gave all the money I earned to my mother. I wanted to contribute to the family household. I also remember going under the boardwalk with my friends to look for coins that people had dropped there. I believe I kept those.

At the high school graduation in 1952, I was named Outstanding Athlete of the Year, earning the Steven Wiesen Memorial Award. I had finally answered the question posed by the "New York Post" the year before about which sport I would choose. I decided to attend Niagara University on a full basketball scholarship. I had scholarships to attend the University of Miami and the University of Pennsylvania. But I wasn't sure I was academically prepared to pass, so I figured if I went to a Catholic school I had a way out.

At Niagara I continued to break track records as a freshman, and I led the junior varsity basketball team in scoring. But then I decided to become a voluntary draftee so I could enlist in the military to fight in the Korean War. I dropped out of Niagara, figuring I could play basketball in the Army. It was a decent plan, I thought. I got a group of my basketball friends to go to Whitehall Street in New York City to enlist.

I was in charge of the bus. I remember my father crying as we pulled out. No one was in better shape than I was; I was sure I was a shoo-in. But in the final physical, the Army rejected me because I had asthma. So I went next door to the Marines. They also told me to get out of there. All the friends I brought with me wound up going, and thankfully they all came back home when the war was over. As for me, I went home to my parents and talked to my high school coach Bobby Gersten, looking for my next step. He made some calls, and in 1954 I got into Rollins College in Winter Park, Florida, where I was once again on a basketball scholarship.

The reason I share my athletic history is that I believe being athletically successful was an important motivation for me. I was always aware that I was participating with others who worked out just as hard as I did. And while I always won, they kept going. I learned to develop an appreciation for people who participate without having to win. They built character just by participating. I respected them and valued that feeling of bonding that comes from sharing a goal with others whether you win or lose. That early experience would serve me well many years later in politics. I didn't always win, but I made sure I approached all issues in a bipartisan way.

The other aspect that matters is the appreciation and love I had for my coaches, which has lasted throughout my life. Each one was important to me, starting with Jimmy McCabe, my high school freshman basketball coach, who was loved by all who worked with him. His brother was Tom McCabe, another mentor whom I will talk about in the next chapter.

Roy Ilowit was my football coach and also the high school wrestling coach. He was a Jewish athlete who played professional football in 1937 with the Brooklyn Dodgers. As my coach, when I was running wind sprints, he was running alongside me. He was an unbelievable athlete. He later was the head football coach at C.W. Post and became athletic director. He was loved and respected by everyone who played for him. Just recently, his daughter stopped me on the boardwalk to greet me. She was visiting the bench I had placed there in his name. I hadn't seen her since she was a little girl. Such are the many connections that have been made in my life.

Bobby Gersten taught me not only how to play varsity basketball, but also how to coach. Because of what I learned from him, as an adult

I was very successful in my coaching in the Catholic Youth Organization (CYO) sports leagues (basketball, baseball, midget football, and swimming) and the East Meadow High School basketball team. Gersten taught me the fundamentals of the sport are the priorities of success. I attribute to him one of the greatest achievements I had when I coached at East Meadow. I had thirteen kids try out for my team who were good athletes but not good basketball players. I taught them the fundamentals I had learned from Gersten and we were very successful. In fact, that year we beat Long Beach in the playoffs. His son became a coach at John F. Kennedy High School in Bellmore, and when East Meadow would play them, I'd have to coach against my former coach's son's team. This was the beginning of many such connections from the people I admired and worked with in Long Beach who would continue to impact my life for years to come—and in unexpected ways.

Irving Gold was my track coach and I loved him dearly. He had a philosophy: Get out in front and stay there and you'll never lose. When I would practice with him, he brought along his Irish setter. He'd say, "Don't worry. Missy doesn't bite." But that damn dog would come after me and nip at my feet. Years later he asked Ellen and me to take care of his dog while his family went on vacation. It was a fat little pug and my kids put dresses on him and played with him. But since he was a little chunky, I took him running with me on the boardwalk. When Irv came back, he said, "What did you do to my dog?" I said, "I got him in shape, Coach."

Decades later, in 2004, I was reminded of where I spent some of my happy early days when the Long Beach School Board dedicated the athletic fields at the Lindell School to me. They also named the Harvey Weisenberg Aquatic and Fitness Center at the Recreation Center. It has been an honor to have a little piece of history in places that had been so significant in my life.

What I can say about all those years is that it was a good life, and it shaped me into the man I am today. But it was just the beginning of what would guide the direction my life would take.

2.

My Early Career

I wasn't at Rollins long before I had to come back to Long Beach. Though he was only in his forties, my father, Big Harry, had a stroke. He was left paralyzed and unable to speak. My mother took care of him as long as she could. Because of his needs, they couldn't stay in the Broadway Apartments anymore, so I bought a house for them in the canals. I had two mortgages and a personal loan of $14,700. Eventually we had to put my father in the Tides Nursing Home, and I'd visit him every night and my sister would too, until he died in 1962. I was with him when he passed, something I am grateful for to this day.

I had always worked as a kid, but now I had to help my parents. I had two jobs. The first I had been doing since I was a teenager, working for the Long Beach Highway Department shoveling coal into the incinerator, helping to fix the streets using a jackhammer, and moving heavy sand. I also worked with good men, like Bill Anderson, who had a special extra-large shovel I liked to borrow. So when I came back from Rollins, this was one of the jobs I returned to. Working with these men helped me to better know the community I lived in. I was a kid working with a diverse group of hard-working men, all with a strong work ethic as they did physical labor for the city. It made an impression on me as I worked alongside them.

I also served as a police officer for the City of Long Beach from 1956 until 1962. In those days all I had to do to get into the force was to take a test. I was on foot patrol, with two walking posts. One was Post 8, which was the North Park area. It was popular with people of color, and over time I got to know and care about the community. My other beat was Post 9 in the West End.

There are newspaper clippings of "daring heroism" from those days that greatly exaggerated my work, including one article in which I was described as twice dashing into a smoky bedroom to save two women who "were frozen to their chairs by panic." There's another story about "two young toughies trying to give the former local high school and college star athlete" a hard time one night. According to the article, I was a rookie cop who picked up one and then the other, threw him to the ground, and then hauled them both off to the station house. While the facts of these stories were all in a day's work, it wasn't quite as dramatic as all that.

I also once helped to save a child who was having a seizure. Many years later Ellen and I were in a supermarket in East Rockaway when a woman came up to me and said, "You don't remember me, but I'll never forget you. I was the little girl you had to give first aid to." It made me smile to hear this, and it was a good reminder of the many ways we can touch other people's lives by the work we choose to do.

I was a good cop, but in the name of trying to set kids on the straight and narrow, I did get into a lot of trouble for disciplining people and then putting them on the train. The way I figured it, you bring them in and lock them up, and then the judge lets them go the next day. So I took care of it with justice on the street. There was a teenage girl who stole a car, so I brought her home and told her father, "Either you take care of disciplining her or I will." Keep in mind that language was a reflection of the times, not something I'd say today. Then detectives from Far Rockaway came down and said, "Where's the person who stole the car?" I told them she ran away. They said they found it hard to believe that a teenage girl could outrun a state quarter-mile champ. Straight-faced, I said, "She was faster than me." I have a lot of police stories to tell. But that's the way I was brought up: If you see something, do something.

I found other ways to accidentally get into trouble, like the time I was on duty and wound up playing stick ball with some kids—one of whom I let wear my police cap—when the police commissioner came by. The commissioner gave me a pass, which was helpful since at the time I was a twenty-three-old working an eight-hour shift at night and going to New York University during the day to get my degree in recreational education.

Thanks to Uncle Buster, who was still City Manager then, we had a terrific recreation program. So I spent whatever free time I had coaching football, baseball, and basketball teams. I even coached a midget football team of boys ages ten to thirteen, sponsored by the Lions Club. I coached the Long Beach midget football team and the CYO St. Mary of the Isle basketball team.

I organized Long Beach hot rod enthusiasts into a club, which was called the Channel Choppers. We put on an auto show and donated the proceeds to Long Beach Hospital. I also ran a Youth Center in Long Beach at the West School.

As a patrolman in 1959, the Long Beach Post #666 and its Ladies Auxiliary of the Jewish War Veterans presented me with their annual "Brotherhood Award." The presentation was made with the cooperation with of the National Conference of Christians and Jews, and included participation of the student body of Long Beach High School.

Though I appreciated the honor, the reason I did all that coaching is that it was important to me that kids learned to respect cops, let alone like them, so that they might think before doing something that would be classified as delinquent. I also wanted them to use their energies in honest recreation.

When I was a kid, the police officers did a lot for me and my friends, particularly Tom McCabe and Joe Hoff. Hoff used to get off his motorcycle and hit fly balls with my friends and me. But it's because of them that I had decided I wanted to be a cop. They were the old-fashioned type of beat patrolmen in whom youngsters could always confide and would always give direct answers. They coached us and told us right from wrong, and if necessary, either gave us a good boot so we couldn't sit down for a couple of days, or else the kind of chewing out that we wouldn't soon forget. We didn't go home to complain to our parents because we knew we deserved it—and besides, we'd probably get worse at home if we told them what had happened.

At the age of twenty-three, I had already determined that much of delinquency was due to a lack of parental interest in what children were doing. I thought the old-time family ties seemed to be missing and parents only became concerned when their kids were in trouble. For a cop to work with and become friends with teenagers was a job in itself. Unfortunately, kids were taught early by their parents that a cop's only job was to arrest you or give you a ticket. And often the first time many kids got to talk to a policeman was when they got into trouble. But the community policing I did at that time, walking Post 8 and Post 9, meant that I was on the streets with the kids, which was an opportunity to interact with them on a positive level. Many of these kids were the ones I also coached at the Recreation Center.

I believe that at the time, Yale Newman and Jimmy McCabe, who both ran the recreation program, were responsible for Long Beach's claim to have the lowest degree of juvenile delinquency for any community of comparable size. They created one of the best recreation programs in the state of New York by really working with every kid who participated. I was glad to be able to be a part of that. I'm proud of my days as a police officer. I still wear my shield number PBA 216 on a ring, and it's also my license plate number.

I earned my Bachelor of Science degree in recreation education from New York University in 1958. I stayed on the police force, becoming president of the Long Beach Police Benevolent Association in 1960. I also did substitute teaching in Bethpage, East Rockaway, and Long Beach. I'd work the midnight-to-eight shift as an officer, and then go to teach. That kind of schedule is definitely made for a much younger man.

In the summer of 1960, I went out to a Native American reservation in Ramona, California, near Warner Hot Springs in San Diego, to teach. I brought my young son Russell with me. I had gotten married to my first wife in 1957 and she wasn't well enough to come. While I was in Ramona, I used to run and work out with Archie Moore, the American professional boxer and the longest reigning World Light Heavyweight champion. I wouldn't go in the ring with him, but he was going to fight Buddy Turman, the American professional heavyweight boxer, and they were training together at this camp. I went in the ring with Turman and he said, "Every time I hit your shoulder would be one on your face." I thought I could handle myself. But after three minutes I couldn't pick my arm up.

In Ramona, I was coaching the kids, and because I was friends with Moore, I coached them in boxing and basketball. I took them to Escondido to play a basketball game, and they didn't want to come out of the locker room because they didn't want to be seen in short pants. It makes me laugh when I remember the boys' faces. But they eventually played games in front of their parents.

My time in California was a good life experience. But my father was then seriously ill, so I had to go back to Long Beach.

At the time, I was also pursuing a Master of Science degree in education from Hofstra University, which I earned in 1962. In 1963, I became a college instructor at Nassau County Community College and taught at Kings Point School in Great Neck, which was a private school for special needs students. I was a teacher and an athletic director of sorts at Kings Point, though that was not really a position. I set up my own physical education program at O'Rourke's Gym in Hempstead, and I held my classes there, teaching health and physical education. I would also take the kids outside and make them run, and when it snowed we'd go sleigh riding. My purpose was to give them a chance to channel their energies. I also taught them the fundamentals of all sports so they could enjoy them not only as a participant, but also so they'd have an understanding when they watched sports and could enjoy the experience better. This involvement came in handy years later when I was a special education teacher in the East Meadow School District.

Loving the ocean as I did, I wanted to be able to give back by saving lives as a lifeguard. I was certified as an ocean lifeguard after taking the lifesaving Red Cross test and then the Nassau County Health Department test. I started a lifeguard career in 1957 that has lasted sixty years. Since 1967, I have served as the Chief Lifeguard Examiner for the City of Long Beach, acting for the Nassau County Department of Health. I just gave my most recent test this June.

I had another summer job around 1962, restaurant owner. I was friends with Lenny Beck, who owned the popular restaurant, Lenny's Steak House on West Beech Street. Lenny also served as a member of the Long Beach City Council in the 1960s. He had followed me as an athlete and as a police officer, so he offered me an opportunity. He was moving into a larger area one block away from his existing restaurant and offered me his restaurant for a dollar. I called it Harvey's Italian Cuisine. We had a pizza oven and Italian dishes made by Lee Jo (Leo Roselli), who owned a bicycle shop on Minnesota Avenue, one block away from Lenny's. We had a great summer business. I'd lifeguard during the day and open up the restaurant at night. The stewardesses from the airlines volunteered as servers and everyone had a good time. It was a happy place.

Sometimes we'd close the doors for private parties. One night a group of men dressed in drag rented out the place. I had many friends who came into my restaurant, and that night since the event was supposed to be private only, I asked them to leave. But some of my male friends tried to pick up the men dressed as women. It was a fun scene to watch. In fact, it was an exciting event, with the men singing and dancing, sharing their talents. The night was a wonderful experience, and I was happy to know my restaurant was the place for so much joy. When I applied for and received a liquor license, I had to give up being a police officer. After about a year and a half, I sold the restaurant to another bar owner in the West End.

During those years, I also earned a physical education certification at Adelphi University, in Garden City, and took courses at the University of Bridgeport for special education certification. Those were busy, but very happy days.

In 1965, I took a civil service test and was appointed Supervisor of Recreation for the City of Long Beach, which was a full-time job. Then I became Recreation Swimming Supervisor, and in 1964, formed the Long Beach Aquatics Swim Team. When I look back on all this I can confirm that basically I worked seven days a week and six nights for many, many years.

What I learned about Long Beach and myself during all those years of working multiple jobs with people of all ages, was the ability to understand the diversity of people's needs. As an athlete and coach, a cop, a lifeguard, and restaurant owner, I had direct contact with a diverse population in Long Beach. This awakened me to the priorities of what is really necessary to have a happy life. Even then, to me every person that I met in Long Beach was like a person in my family. They became a part of my life and to this day I still feel that way. All this was before I met Ellen and my life changed in ways I never expected—but welcomed.

3

Meeting Ellen

In 1965, among the many jobs I held was being in charge of the lifeguards at the Coral Reef Beach Club. I was paid, but also had the benefit of access to a cabana for my family, including my sister Brenda and her children. That's also when I was Long Beach Recreation Swimming Supervisor. One of the program activities I was in charge of was holding swim competitions, including the women's swim event. Among those who wanted to compete was a graceful woman I had become friends with, Ellen Laufer.

When I had first spotted Ellen at the pool, I swore I had to know her better. I also bet a friend fifty cents that I would take her out on a date. I don't remember if I ever collected on that bet, but I did learn later that though I had thought it was all my idea, my friend had a hand in putting us together. At the time, I was separated from my first wife and a single parent to my two young sons Russell, then age five, and Gregg, age two. Though it was rare for a father in those days, I always had my kids at work with me, because Long Beach Recreation was two blocks away from my house.

When Ellen first spoke to me about entering the race, I explained with mock seriousness that it would be very difficult; her competition consisted of someone who had just learned to swim and a very pregnant woman. So we laughed together for the first time.

Willowy, with a magnificent, sculpted face, and a sparkling smile, Ellen could have been a fashion model or a movie star. She spoke in soft, elegant tones. Her words demonstrated an intellect I did not imagine I could match. But that didn't stop me from trying. Everyone who ever met her admired her because she was just an exceptional person. To this day people tell me stories that they met her once and they never forgot her. Even when she was ill in her last days, she asked the doctor if he was okay. She was such a special person.

Back in 1965, when this very beautiful young woman won the race handily, I looked for an excuse to see her again. Due to a delay in shipment, I did not have a trophy to present to Ellen. I did have one left over from 1964, so I asked if she would accept a year-old trophy. She said, "Sure." I looked into her hazel-green eyes and saw something very special. That young woman would later become my wife. But of course neither of us knew it that sunny summer day.

Ellen, who was a registered nurse, had three children, including two girls, Julie and Vicki, who were the same ages as my sons. She also had Ricky, her special child. He had been born five years earlier with cerebral palsy that was so severe that in the language of the day he was called "profoundly mentally retarded." He could not speak or cry. He couldn't feed himself, and at age five was still in diapers. He had also been born with a clubfoot that was never completely remediated by surgery or other interventions.

Looking back, I truly feel that God put Ellen—and Ricky—in my life. That was when I was taking courses in special education at the University of Bridgeport in Connecticut so I could get my certification, which helped me to understand the needs of special children and their parents. Ellen and I became friends because of my interest in children with developmental disabilities.

At the core of our friendship was an enormous respect for this woman who provided so much love and nurturing to her children, which she then extended to mine. It was a relationship I feel was made in heaven. We both had our challenges, of course. My first wife had addiction and mental health problems, and for the protection of our sons, I had gone to court to obtain sole custody of Russell and Gregg. Ellen's husband had wanted to institutionalize Ricky since he was an infant. She fought to keep Ricky home. But over time she was also raising two little girls and coping with a recent diagnosis of type 1 diabetes, so she conceded. She could not keep him home any longer.

Ultimately, Ellen showed me what it was like to mother Ricky. The compassion and courage she mustered for her son only made me love her more. It also made me want to change the world for her. She inspired me to eventually do the work that made me one of the most prominent legislators in New York State. But long before I entered politics, we were a young couple in love.

I was also a man who fell in love twice when Ellen invited me to meet Ricky at the municipal indoor pool in Long Beach on June 4, 1966. Before she could commit to me, Ellen felt she had to show me what I would face in helping to raise Ricky, if our romance blossomed. When I was going to meet Ricky that first time, I was concerned. I wasn't afraid of much, but I sensed Ellen's fear. Fortunately, she had faith. That first time, Ellen and I walked up to Ricky from behind. He turned at the sound of her voice. He smiled a smile like you've never seen. It was full of love and joy and happiness. I'd never seen anything like it. I was already falling in love with Ellen, but that smile, Ricky's smile, that was the final shove. I believed in that moment if Ellen could make her child that happy, perhaps she could do the same for me. I would prove to be right for the rest of our years together.

That day I watched Ricky splash, as best as the boy could. I reached out to help him float. Suddenly Ricky calmed, smiled, and squeezed my hand. And that was it. Ellen beamed with gratitude and our love story of being each other's support and champions was sealed. Of course the challenges Ricky faced were enormous.

We became a couple who had a Brady Bunch-like combination of children to raise. They were like two sets of twins. Julie and Russell are a month apart, and Gregg and Vicki are two months apart. That year we took the boys and girls to many different places together. There's a pond in Baldwin where we went with our children and fed the geese. We also took vacations to Puerto Rico, to the mountains in upstate New York, and to Florida. We always travelled as a family. We spent most of our time together and eventually decided to look for a house.

We found a two-family home on Pine Street that had been custom-built. The price was more than I could afford at that time, but the owner had been injured so could no longer live there. She called to say her house was available at a price that worked for me. So we bought the house, got married on August 3, 1967, and set up housekeeping together. The new household had four children, Ellen's daughters and my sons. Although Ricky then lived in a facility for the disabled, he was a frequent visitor and a constant, overwhelming presence in our lives.

Vicki, Ellen's younger daughter, said a few years ago that in looking back there was substantial jealousy among the four of them because everything revolved around Ricky. She said, "There was the three of them, Mom, Harvey, and Ricky. The rest of us were secondary."

Of course all the kids were important to us. Ellen and I had a strong relationship and we agreed our marriage came first. We thought we were setting an example about how two people can really care for each other, not realizing how that could impact the kids, making them feel that we weren't as available to them as we thought we were. As parents you make decisions that seem right at the time, but it's impossible not to make mistakes.

As for Ricky, for me, his disabilities made him easy to love. He is still incapable of doing anything wrong. Meanwhile, in our somewhat chaotic household of four overcharged young children who became teenagers who could sometimes be less than angelic, there were the typical arguments and disagreements. They were all very involved in sports, including being on swim teams, so we were always running around with one or all of them. It was something we did as a family, with each sibling supporting the other by cheering on the sidelines with me and Ellen. My sister Brenda remembers thinking that Ellen had a quite a handful to deal with. She said she recalls going to support Russell in a swim meet in White Plains and seeing Ellen with a big basket. While she was watching the swim meet, she was mending the kids' socks.

At the same time, anything Ricky did, like a bathroom issue, creating a racket, snatching food off someone else's plate—how could we find fault? You just couldn't get angry at him. If he did something negative, it was only because of his medical condition. A disabled child is perfect; he is incapable of meaning to do anything wrong. He gives unconditional love and that is easy to reciprocate.

Besides, the natural resentment of our other four is perhaps overstated. I doted on my sons, Russell and Gregg, serving as a coach for their football, basketball, and swimming teams. Ellen doted on her gifted girls Julie and Vicki, making sure they had their fill of art and music lessons. Together our days—and many nights—were filled with being present for all four growing kids for their many activities. We were both devoted parents.

After I met Ellen, I went on to become a more focused special education teacher. After working part-time at Nassau County Community College, I worked in the East Meadow School District from 1967 to

1989. I started out teaching driver's education, and when they did away with the program, I went into special education at the elementary level. One year I was offered the principal's job by the East Meadow School Board, but I turned it down because I didn't want to give up teaching my special education kids. Later I became an assistant principal in that district.

We were also a dual-income family, since Ellen continued to work at Long Beach Hospital and as a school nurse at St. Joseph's (where she was the only Jewish nurse). Later she worked at Bayview Nursing Home in Island Park. But she was always home for dinner with the kids. We ate every dinner together as a family.

I also continued my tradition established as a police officer of coaching sports. Among the kids I coached were my boys Russell and Gregg. They were in junior high in Long Beach where the atmosphere in the 1970s was challenging for young men. I wanted to have them in the East Meadow School District with me, so I paid tuition for them. I had the ability to coach them and I thought being in high school there would be a better opportunity for them to be successful. The girls stayed in Long Beach. Our family did what many do, making tough decisions based on our individual kid's needs.

In a *New York Post* article from January 18, 1978, the boys were called East Meadow High School's basketball stars. I was the head basketball coach, and sitting on the bench with me was Ellen, whom the paper called "the head counselor and cheerleader." Ellen had started sitting on the bench when I became the school's head basketball coach in 1973, making it a family operation.

By the time of that article, Russell was a heavily recruited power forward, and Gregg, a high-scoring point guard. Russell played lacrosse and basketball. He had played football in junior high for Long Beach, before going to East Meadow. He was an all-star basketball champion for the South Shore and was named MVP in a regional all-star game for Jewish high school boys sponsored by Yeshiva University. As a young boy, he was among the nation's top ten in two events in his age-group for swimming, and he won the Long Beach Punt, Pass & Kick competition six straight years, from ages eight through thirteen. Gregg was an outstanding running back and defensive player in East Meadow. He went back to Long Beach for his last two years of high school, and became an outstanding defensive football player on Long Island.

Meanwhile, the girls, Julie and Vicki, not only joined us on the bench to cheer on their brothers, they were busy themselves. They took piano lessons. Julie was a talented artist, and Vicki a talented musician with an exceptional singing ability. At one time or another, all four kids were lifeguards. In fact, we were always together during the summer. I worked at the beach clubs where I was in charge of the lifeguards. Ellen was the nurse, and Julie, Russell, Gregg, and Vicki all worked as lifeguards. We were in many ways a typically busy Long Island family that did many activities together. All too soon Julie, Russell, Gregg, and Vicki all went off to college, married, and settled into adulthood, and eventually parenthood, making Ellen and me proud. There are six grandchildren in our family now as well.

Nevertheless, when you have a special needs child, they're always at the forefront. I don't think the others ever fully understood just how much Ricky needed from us. We were always there for the others, but nothing gave me greater joy than providing Ricky with a "happy day," when he was able to do the everyday tasks that typically abled children do without a thought, like toileting. Families with special needs children understand the joy that comes from their child's achievements, which are no less important than those of their abled children, but often come at much greater cost and challenge. It was Ricky who first taught me these lessons.

Throughout our fifty years together, we wrote love notes to each other, sometimes daily, and left them around the house for each to find. Some were mailed when we were forced to be apart. Though it can be painful for me to read them now, there are some I want to share here as a testament to how much we loved each other.

November 11, 1977

My Dear Wife,

I appreciate you, my dear wife. You bring such complete happiness to my life.
Your love and efforts are always there. I realize your chores are beyond compare.
Your great efficiency and mobility is only matched by your love-giving ability.

*I adore your wonderful face. Your beauty lights up every place,
wherever you may go. People always smile and say hello. You
are such a precious delight that I thank God I may hold you
each night. Your warmth and love remind me to thank
God above!*
I just want you to know, that your husband loves you so.

H

June 15, 1981

My Dearest Ellen,

*Happy Birthday—with all my love. You are more beautiful today than
ever before. You are the most wonderful wife a man can have. You make
me proud to be your partner. I appreciate and adore you. But most of
all, respect and admire you for your great talents and intelligence. You
are a most beautiful and complete person and I deeply love you. Have
a happy day.*

All my love,
Harv

Sept. 17, 1981

My Dearest Ellen,

*I have a few minutes of free time and I want to tell you how much
I love and appreciate you. You are so very beautiful, capable, and
efficient that I admire and desire you on a daily basis. You have given
me so much pleasure and have made my life so much more enjoyable.
It is your support and nearness that makes each day enjoyable,
especially the nearness of each night and delight of holding you close.
I thank you for being such a good wife and for your interest in our
home and for always helping me whenever I need you. I wish you
to know that I truly love you and that you are the sunlight of each
day. In closing, remember that I respect, appreciate, and most of all
desire your friendship always. I hope you have a good day! Every day
I love you.*

Your Pal,
H

January 8, 1985

My Dearest El,

*I love you and I miss you when we are apart. I'm just taking a minute
to tell you I appreciate and love you each day of my life.
With all my love,*

H

January 2, 1986

My Dearest El,

*A New Year is here and I'm another year older (but better). I want to
share with you just how much I love you, and how deep my feelings
are for you. I want you to always be aware how much I appreciate all
you do for me and how much I enjoy our closeness. This is the true
joy of my life—just being together. Where we live is unimportant,
but as long as we are together, I will be happy. All I need is our bed—
bathroom—food and you. And if the ocean is there, that's a plus. I'm
looking forward to getting home and holding you—as always!
Just know I love you.*

*Your,
H*

June 15, 1988

My Dearest Ellen,

*Better than a card with someone else writing my thoughts or feelings,
I am writing to you my beautiful, wonderful wife. More than twenty
years of "being together" has given me all the happiness a person can
ask for. You are still the most competent, efficient, and loving wife.
You are the most beautiful, sexy, and delicious woman in the world,
and I still enjoy just looking at you, being with you, and most of all
holding you. I love you and wish you a very happy birthday and as
your present, I will be your slave for the day!!
I love you my wife.*

*Love,
H*

Undated

My Dearest Wife,

I wish you all that you desire. I dedicate my life to give you every happiness you desire, but most of all I give you my total devoted love. I so appreciate all the caring and love you have given me. I return all my love, body and mind to you. You are my entire joy and pleasure and my best friend. I love you on this your birthday and on all other days.

Yours for a lifetime,
You husband,
Me

June 15, 1991 (on Assembly letterhead)

My Dearest Ellen,

I wish you a happy, happy birthday. I must tell you that with each year together you get more beautiful and my love and respect grows more intense. I could never express my appreciation for the super-wonderful human being you are, and how proud I am to have you as my wife. I wish you a very happy birthday and I love you with all my heart always!

Your loving husband,
H

Undated (on a grocer list)

My dear and wonderful husband,

Words cannot express how very much I love you. Really, Harvey, you are the best and most wonderful husband in this whole world. I am so lucky and blessed. I'm waiting patiently for you.

Your El, always, with love

Tuesday

Harvey dearest,

Words cannot express my feelings for you. You are my only asset! I love you, Harv—I emos, would die without you. (Please don't try me!) Harvey, you are one-in-a-million and I am so, so lucky to have you as my beloved husband. Every day loving you more & more.

Your only, El

August 3, 1992

My dearest Harvey,

I cannot believe we are married 25 years. I am so truly blessed to have you not only as my husband, but as my very best (and only) friend. You are a magnificent man! Wonderful in every way. How can I ever thank you for being such a perfect and loving husband? (Yes, I know!) Do you like this card? Well we all do change—but you have only gotten better! I love you with all my heart and body, my dear, sweet, wonderful husband. I pray we have each other for many more happy years. I am grateful for each day I can spend with you. You are my life and my love. Happy anniversary # 25, Harv, dearest.

I love you always.
Kisses and hugs,
Your El

December 30, 2008 (Assembly letterhead)

My Darling Husband Harvey,

Words could never express how I feel about you. You are my life and my everlasting love. You have given me everything I could ever imagine. Your love means everything to me. Your kindness, your patience, your thoughtfulness, your love of all of our children, especially Ricky with his special needs. You are always there for all of us. I wish you the best & happiest 75th birthday ever! Tomorrow will be a very wonderful day. I love you with all my heart—today, tomorrow & always.

Your devoted wife,
Ellen

There are many more letters, especially for our fortieth and fiftieth anniversaries, but I have put them away for safekeeping. It has been fifty years of total love and appreciation.

Me at age three with my mother and father, Renee and Harry, enjoying the sands of Long Beach—a place I fell in love with.

Long Beach High School basketball team in 1948. I'm number five.

Long Beach High School relay team in 1951. I'm number seventeen.

My police officer days in Long Beach helped me to better understand the needs of the people I would eventually serve there as a council member.

The CYO basketball team I coached at St. Mary of the Isle Church.
I'm on the left and Father Frances Conlon is on the right.

Ellen and me early in our relationship, which included the beach, of course.

Our blended family in the sixties: Ellen and me with Russell and Julie (middle row) and Vicki and Gregg (front).

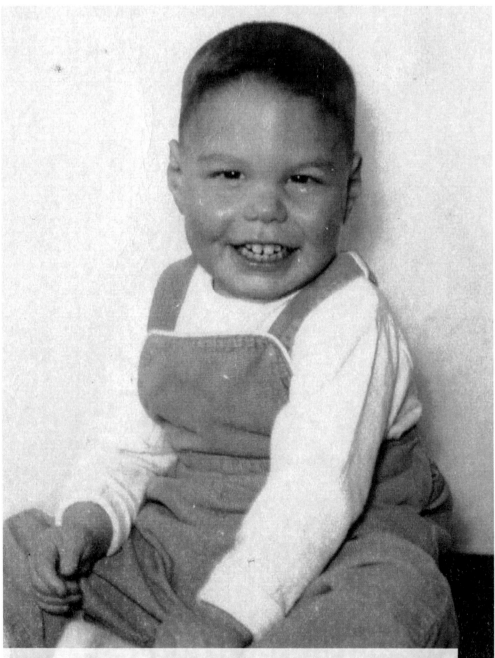

Ricky as a baby with the same sweet face that draws people to him today.

4.

Raising Ricky

During the late spring of 1958, twenty-three-year-old Ellen Laufer, a registered nurse who had earned a Bachelor of Science degree from Adelphi College, awaited the birth of her first child with great anticipation. She lived in North Bellmore with her husband, Jerry Laufer. Because it was the late 1950s, she was planning to give up her nursing job to become a stay-at-home mother. In an account of this time that she wrote many years later, she said she had been brimming with hope. When she first held her newborn on June 3, she saw nothing wrong beyond his left club foot. She viewed the bundle in her arms as perfect.

One of the details she wrote later about those early days proved to be true. "The doctors put a cast on his leg, which was how the condition was treated in that era. My strong little fighter kicked the cast off later that same evening and it had to be re-set. I viewed it as a good sign and although I didn't know it at the time, it was a harbinger of Ricky's life and his fight to survive in a world that was wrought with challenges."

Soon, however, her instincts as a mother and a nurse told her that Eric Mitchell Laufer, nicknamed "Toodles" and later Ricky, wasn't developing as he should. He didn't cry and couldn't hold his head up unsupported. At three months old he had a series of seizures. Although she sought medical attention, there was a prevalent "wait and see" approach. She wrote that the doctors told her in blunt terms this meant a child wouldn't be labeled "retarded" until at least six months. One neurologist expressed the opinion that Ricky would outgrow the spasms. Medical professionals used words like "retardation" and "cerebral palsy," but no actual diagnosis was made. Given the stigma of those decades, and the future prospects of one labeled thus, Ellen conceded in her retelling that she supposed this made sense at the time.

Her fears were confirmed within Ricky's first year when he was diagnosed with cerebral palsy. As is still so often the case with disabled children, it was difficult for the medical profession to clarify what was wrong, or to offer the new parents any assurances. In fact, Ellen wrote that the "doctor sat with me and explained that Ricky might never walk, talk, or amount to anything and would be like a `vegetable,' incapable of learning and would require custodial care only. In the misguided era's attempt at being kind in the face of my obvious reluctance to give up my child, I was further warned that it wouldn't be fair to my other, future children, and that I should institutionalize him as soon as possible before I `became too attached'!" She was also told that Ricky needed to "be put somewhere so that we and the people close to us would not be embarrassed by his appearance or burdened by his care."

Ellen recorded copious details of Ricky's early life in a classic "baby book," marketed to mothers and first published in 1928, *Our Baby's First Seven Years: A Record Book Which Will Prove of Value to Parent, Doctor and School as Child Grows to Maturity*. She wrote in it for longer than seven years, cramming it with notes peppered with medical and motherly observations. These journals serve as crucial historical notes for how Ellen's life was upended by the birth of a disabled child—and how devoted she was to him regardless. They also served for her—and for me when I read them—as a clarion call for more programs and increased funding for the disabled. These remain as crucial issues to this day when Medicaid and other cuts are always on the table.

Being the positive, loving person she was, Ellen noted the highlights of Ricky's smallest of accomplishments, rather than lament the series of missed milestones. For example, in September 1961, she wrote, "3 years, 5 months = REAL PROGRESS!! For six days now Ricky has been pulling himself up to standing position in bed, on the floor, anywhere. . . he's crawling all over the floor." When Ricky was six, she wrote, "July 1964: able to walk many steps alone."

There are notes about birthday parties he attended, including one where he and baby sister Julie wore matching outfits in June 1961. And an outing to Howard Johnson's on Hempstead Turnpike that summer, followed by a walk in Salisbury Park where he and Julie played on the swings. These are all details that would otherwise indicate a typical childhood.

There are also notes for a "daytime sitter" in 1963 that gave an attuned mother's instructions, not only about what Ricky would need but also about Julie and infant Vicki. She reassured the sitter that five-year-old Ricky likes to chew on his toys and "especially on the chain of little red pocketbook."

But the dark side was that almost from birth Ricky's father wanted to institutionalize him. He wasn't the only one who was insisting. Many relatives and friends told Ellen that "everyone" would be better off if Ricky was institutionalized—and thereby allowed to fade in their memories. Eventually Ellen's and Jerry's marriage was destroyed over this conflict. Ellen wanted to love and care for her child herself—and she feared what would happen if she had to let someone else do it instead. She wrote: "He was beautiful and perfect to me. Who would care for my non-verbal, vulnerable baby better than I did? If I put Ricky into the care of strangers, who would love him? Who would kiss him, rock him and sing to him? Who would anticipate his needs? How would any caregiver really know and bond with Ricky?"

Her fears and the fears of so many other parents like her turned out to be terribly accurate. But for Ricky's first five years, Ellen poured all her love and nurse's training into caring for her precious child. She wrote, "I decided to take the more difficult path and kept Ricky home. Thus began a time of great struggle…" She was referring to juggling caring for Ricky and her two girls, while her parents, who had been a great support to her, moved to Florida.

At first she hoped that a good compromise would be to find a school for Ricky where during the day he could receive care and, with any luck, some education, while he continued to live at home. In 1962, she sent him to the United Cerebral Palsy (UCP) Association of Nassau County in Roosevelt. In those days it was abysmal because there were no real programs, interventions, or therapy. "For three hours five days a week Ricky sat strapped to a wheelchair and stared at nothing," Ellen wrote in the baby book. She only allowed him to stay there from September until November.

Ellen said that while Ricky didn't get much from his time at UCP, she did get to meet other parents who shared her struggles. She vividly remembered meeting a mother of a thirteen-year-old girl. "Her forlorn, resentful expression spoke in volumes as she shared how, like me, she had been determined to keep her daughter home and did so for thirteen years. She strongly discouraged me from doing what she did as it had `ruined her life.' Her family had disowned her, her husband left her, and no one would socialize with her because she was always with her child. I will never forget her, because she was a reflection of what I would become if I continued to resist the tide of growing sentiment to give up my child. It took another three years before I would give up the struggle."

When Ricky turned five, Ellen realized the time had come to give in to her husband's demand. By then Julie was four and Vicki only a year. Ellen had developed type 1 diabetes, also known as juvenile diabetes, which meant she was insulin dependent and required constant medical vigilance to maintain her own health. Today, though type 1 diabetes is still a serious and chronic illness, those who have it also have access to better medical advances to maintain healthy blood sugar levels. But in the early 1960s, it required that Ellen boil syringes and needles in order to give herself insulin, and test her urine in a complicated procedure that required a Bunsen burner, not to mention being attentive to what she ate. Low blood sugars could mean she could faint, and high blood sugars could make her seriously ill. Self-care as a diabetic was already a challenge, without adding in two little girls and a special needs child who could not speak or feed himself. Ellen was also working full-time as a nurse. I can't even imagine how she was handling all that stress while her marriage was also disintegrating over Ricky's care.

Ellen chronicled some of her emotional struggles about this time. "On several occasions," she wrote in Ricky's baby book, "I was invited to social events with my friends and my 'normal' kids, but was told in no uncertain terms that Ricky was not welcome. Ricky's father wanted him sent away and this disagreement would eventually destroy my marriage. When I was diagnosed with diabetes, I knew I could not continue as things were. I had come to the sad realization that I could no longer be Ricky's sole caretaker when I was losing the rest of my family and my health. . ."

She continued: "In 1963 I was ready to concede a bitter defeat. Ricky had turned five. His peers were going to kindergarten and doing the things that normal five-year-olds do. Making friends, learning some letters and numbers, running, skipping, jumping ropes. Ricky was still very much a baby, and the difference between him and his peers was starkly obvious and increasing every day. I was ready to admit my limits and knew I couldn't walk this path alone any longer."

What Ellen experienced as a parent of a young special needs child is the similar heartbreak that she and I heard over and over again in our advocacy work years later. The difference today is that there are more medical advancements and early intervention services for children, as well as support systems. Though things are still not perfect—and I explore in my account all the many ways problems remain—what Ellen went through all those years ago taught her how to be there for the many parents we encountered along the way. It also enabled her to be my teacher about all the things special needs children and families need.

Sending Ricky away broke her heart but not her will. At the time the only available institutions in New York were Willowbrook State Psychiatric Hospital in Staten Island and Wassaic State School in Amenia, which is in upstate New York. Naturally Ellen wanted to look at the one closest to home. Ellen had already visited Willowbrook, where doctors showed her only the sanitized wards, not the rest of the facility. But as an alert mother, she had already made a determination that others would make over the next several years about what they were trying to hide. She wrote in his baby book on September 21, 1961, "Not a place for Ricky." Willowbrook would later go down in history as the embodiment of America's failure in dealing with the disabled, a hellhole where children were manacled and allowed to wallow in their own waste for hours and days at a time. In fact, it became the subject of investigations after State Senator Robert Kennedy toured there just a few years after Ellen did in 1965, and he found the residents to be living in horrible conditions.

That left Ellen with Wassaic when she was finally ready to make a decision a few years later. Though not as horrific as Willowbrook, it was awful nevertheless. When Ricky was taken to Wassaic on August 29, 1963, he weighed about fifty-two pounds. Ellen was directed to leave him there for his total care and not to return for six weeks so Ricky could adjust to his new environment.

Six weeks later, Ellen went back and found that her five-year-old son had lost weight and was no longer smiling. She gave it more time. He was supposed to come home for a visit at Christmas, but her girls had chicken pox, so the visit was delayed until January 2, 1964. By then he weighed less than half his original body weight (though the hospital had kept many diapers on him to make him appear in better condition than he was). Ricky was starved almost to death. He had a black tongue, was bent over, and looked like he had been in a concentration camp. He had developed the ability to regurgitate any food he had so he could eat it again, which devastated his digestive system. The acid not only damaged his organs, but also his teeth, which all had to be removed. And through it all he was not able to express his pain or discomfort. What a horror for any parent and child to go through. That it happened to my Ellen and Ricky still breaks my heart. Ellen immediately took him to the family pediatrician. When the doctor saw Ricky, he cried. Ricky was admitted to Long Island Jewish Hospital, where he stayed for almost two weeks.

Ellen nursed him back to health over the next several months. She again had to make a decision, because despite what Ricky had lived through the situation at home hadn't changed. She still had two other children and Ricky still needed round-the-clock care. After much research, she took Ricky to the Allegheny School in Pittsburgh, Pennsylvania in November 1964. Before she did, she wrote, "I pray to God he will survive there—please— and do well. Let the people there be kind and loving to our dear Ricky for he is such a sweet angel. He only deserves to be loved and well-cared for, for he can hurt no one. I must feel grateful to be able to have loved him for six years… Dear God, let his new home be loving."

Though Ellen left her visits with Ricky at the Allegheny School feeling more positive about his care most of the time, it was there that Ricky was placed in a scalding tub and was severely burned. He wound up with a temperature of over 106 degrees. He almost died and was hospitalized in Pittsburgh. He recovered and stayed at Allegheny.

On a supplementary paper in the baby book, on June 4, 1965, Ellen wrote about Ricky's visit home from that institution. He slept in a crib in the living room. Amidst other details are two very telling sentences. "I took him swimming in the Long Beach indoor pool and he adored it. This was the 1st time Harvey saw him."

When Ellen and I were married in 1967, we sought a resource closer to home, so Ellen would have more access to then nine-year-old Ricky. We contacted our State Assemblyman, Jerry Kremer, to seek placement at the Long Island Developmental Center in Melville, New York, so we would be able to oversee and visit Ricky frequently.

By then my warrior side had emerged. I defied orders to stay away, and forced institutions to explain themselves, forced them to treat Ricky humanely. Decades before I officially adopted Ricky in 2010, I made it clear that no one would abuse my son and get away with it.

In his life, Ricky has lived at four institutions in New York and Pennsylvania, including the Long Island Developmental Center in Melville, and the Helen Kaplan Program House in Plainview, run by the AHRC Nassau, where he still resides. Some were better than others. On the surface they were all better than Willowbrook. Yet, he suffered some form of neglect and abuse almost everywhere he was placed. Ellen was often asked to stay away so Ricky could acclimate to living apart from her. She returned sooner than suggested, and yet was never there when the abuse and neglect occurred—because it rarely does when family is around. In every instance Ellen and/or I reacted as quickly as we could when either we were told outright about these incidents or found them out from caring staff.

Through it all, Ricky, so much like Ellen, never exhibited any aggression, but smiled, had an awareness he was loved, and gave love by just holding her hand and laying his head on her shoulder. Ricky understood what was happening when people were going to diaper and dress him, because he would cooperate. He was a pleasure to care for, which many direct caregivers have voiced, all through the years.

Ricky has always loved music. We took him to concerts every summer on the Long Beach boardwalk. People enjoyed seeing him rock to the music in his wheelchair. He also enjoys flowers and water. But most of all, he loves to eat. He loved his food, and Ellen always presented everything he liked best. His food had to be pureed and fed to him, which took a great deal of time and much care. But Ellen was happy to do this for him.

Ellen was attentive to Ricky while he was at the institutions where he resided and during home visits, while being a mother to all of our other children. Being a nurse, she could anticipate, diagnose, and treat Ricky. She had an instinct, as many parents might have, that he was going to sneeze before he sneezed. She knew by his movements what Ricky wanted or needed, and she was a caregiver who gave so much love and attention.

Ricky is a special angel, and only gives happiness with all the effort to maintain his well-being. He gives more happiness than the effort to care for him. To know Ricky is to love him, just as to know Ellen was to love her.

Whenever we came to visit Ricky, as soon as he saw Ellen, he would jump up and dance and turn in circles. To this day, when I visit Ricky and I speak to him, he stops what he's doing and smiles and puts his hands out. He knows I am there, and he knows that I am going to give him love.

Most recently, we have had what I can only refer to as a miraculous development, caused, in all honesty, by Ricky. Our daughter Vicki has always loved her brother, but she had been distracted by other aspects of her life. Vicki has made great improvements in her life and has begun visiting Ricky regularly with me. She holds his hand, feeds him, and feels his love when he puts his head on her shoulder. She is an important part of her brother's life, and feeling Ricky's love has brought her so much happiness.

Ricky may not understand all the nuances that have impacted his care during his sixty years. He communicates as he always has, with grunts and smiles instead of speech. He cannot swallow whole foods. He can walk only with assistance, and needs to wear a diaper. He is now blind because he injured his head while dealing with abdominal pain he had no way to communicate to us. But he has always expressed his gratitude, from the moment I met that young boy and helped him in the same surf as my childhood. Ricky tells me he loves me by squeezing my hand or putting his head on my shoulder.

He probably doesn't realize that caring for and helping to raise him from that first summer I met him and Ellen led me to spend the rest of my life advocating, not only for Ricky, but for all the other special needs children and adults I have been able to reach. He has been an extraordinary blessing to our family. He makes us realize what love is all about. He radiates warmth to us. Perhaps most important, he makes us realize how important it is to be aware of vulnerable people who are often neglected or kept out of sight.

Both Ellen and I became advocates for people with special needs. Over the years we became active supporters for research on cerebral palsy and autism, as well as champions of better care and education for all children with disabilities. When I entered local politics—first on the City Council and then in the State Assembly—the needs of these children became my most passionate cause. It is because of Ellen and Ricky that my career path ever came to be. For much of it, Ellen was by my side, advocating for children just like Ricky—and the parents who loved them.

I formally adopted Ricky in 2010. I was seventy-four and in good health. But it seemed wise to start putting my life in order. Of importance to me was formalizing the role Ricky and I had had for decades; father and son. Though it seemed like it should be an easy process, there were several steps to take along the way. For one thing, Ricky's birth father needed to be approached. Jerome Laufer, a retired furniture executive, was by then retired and living in Florida. He hadn't seen Ricky in more than forty years, and hadn't even inquired about him when he talked with his daughters, Julie and Vicki. But he could have filed an objection simply out of pique. Any objection could have been a major roadblock.

And although my political position made me a force in Albany, decisions are made on a county level in New York at Surrogates Court. I had to go through the same process as any other prospective adoptive parent. Nassau County had only one Surrogate Judge, the Honorable John B. Riordan. By then, Riordan had been on the bench for more than a decade. He appointed a local lawyer, Phyllisann Polizzi Kalenka, to conduct an investigation to determine if the proposed adoption was in Ricky's best interests.

Ours was a tricky assignment. New York law requires that adult children consent to being adopted. Ricky could not speak. Parents of disabled children, especially nonverbal children, develop a private language that allows them to divine what their offspring wants. The parents can translate facial tics or waving hands to read moods, correctly guess desire, identify fears and dislikes. Ellen and I had mastered that special language. We knew what Ricky wanted, whether it was a special meal or a ride in the car. But now we had to hope we could somehow translate that nonverbal language to the lawyer and judge. As *"guardian ad litem,"* Phyllisann referred to Ricky as her "ward" and used his given name, Eric Mitchell Laufer.

Phyllisann first met Ricky on December 29, 2009, visiting him at his residence, the Helen Kaplan Program House in Plainview. "Eric shares a very large bedroom with another resident and both individuals have more than adequate personal space," Phyllisann wrote in her report to Judge Riordan. "The bedroom is bright and clean, yet decorated in much the same manner as a bedroom in a private home would be. . ... I was most impressed by the design and maintenance of the group home wherein Eric resides, and was particularly glad to witness the caring interchange between staff and residents."

Phyllisann had interviewed us by phone and talked to a number of other friends. Following her tour of Ricky's residence came the first meeting with us. "We traveled from the group home to a nearby Burger King restaurant, which Eric enjoys visiting and which possesses sufficient space for Mr. and Mrs. Weisenberg to care for Eric during the meal," Phyllisann wrote.

It was a routine visit for us, but must have been unusual for Phyllisann. Ricky requires specially pureed food and would have choked on a Whopper or fries. But he liked the outing. It was a break from the residence, a place with plenty of room for his wheelchair. And it was the kind of "normal" place that those who are severely disabled too often do not get to visit. When it was time to clean him up, I got him to lean against the sink. I removed his trousers and his dirty diaper. I talked to him the whole time, thanking him for cooperating, and thanking him for making it easier on me. He smiled and laughed the whole time. I don't need to tell you what it's like to change the diaper of a grown man.

We eventually took Ricky back to his group home. Phyllisann returned to her office to complete the report in the case she titled "In the Matter of the Adoption of a Child Whose First Name is Eric—file 45974." She wrote: "The happiness expressed on his face was accompanied by a gleeful uplifting of his arms when each parent approached to hug him. He returned their embrace with much excitement." She described the lunch of pureed and liquefied food. "Eric ate abundantly and when he had finished, had eaten the equivalent of a well-balanced lunch consisting of a sandwich, soup, fruit, a dessert, and hot chocolate."

At least Phyllisann was sold. We still had to deal with Ricky's father. Although Phyllisann had determined that Laufer had "abandoned his parental right and obligations [that would] eliminate the need for his consent," she still sent off a FedEx package containing a pile of legal documents to Laufer, asking if he would waive his right to fight the proposed adoption.

Her report made it clear that regardless of what Laufer said, her mind was already made up. She wrote that even in "the absence of a formal order of adoption, Eric and Mr. Weisenberg will continue to consider themselves father and son. The relationship between the two individuals is one of unconditional love and concern."

As it happened, Ricky's father signed the papers, ceding his right to challenge the adoption without explanation. Shortly before he died in 2017, Laufer called me and thanked me for raising all three of his children.

There was a final issue: Ellen wanted to change Ricky's legal name to the one he was known by. Phyllisann agreed: "Although this report refers to my ward as Eric, based on my observations when I met with Eric and Mr. and Mrs. Weisenberg, he responds to the name of 'Ricky.' Furthermore, it appears that persons outside his family [including] the staff and residents of Eric's group home, also refer to him as Ricky. As for the legal change of Eric's surname, I also foresee no problem with such action. Based on what I have observed, Eric considers Mr. and Mrs. Weisenberg to be his parents and, consequently, this change should present no complication for him."

And so, on April 19, 2010, Ellen and I drove to the AHRC residence to get Eric, relatively certain that he would emerge from the court as Ricky. The proceeding was short. Judge Riordan summarized Phyllisann's report. The adoption was official. Several minutes later, the judge in his black robes posed for a photo with us. Ricky Weisenberg was officially my son.

Yesterday I was with Ricky. I was holding him and he put his face next to mine. I broke down crying. I felt his love and our connection to Ellen. He still inspires me to fight for his rights and the rights of all families who need an advocate. Raising Ricky has been my great honor and privilege.

5.

Early Public Life— Long Beach City Council

By 1974 I had already been working as a special education teacher in the East Meadow School District for a few years, and I was coaching basketball there. Ellen was still working as a full-time nurse, first at Long Beach Hospital, then as a school nurse and private duty nurse. Together we were raising four children in their early teens, as well as making sure that Ricky received the care and attention he needed in his group home, Long Island Developmental Center in Melville. We were a busy family. So why did I decide that year to run for Long Beach City Councilman, my first foray into public life?

I was founder and president of the Central Homeowners Association, which represented people from Magnolia Boulevard to Lafayette Boulevard. (Later it was expanded to a Combined Civic Association to represent the leaders of all community civic associations.) I also spoke up at City Council meetings. The city of my youth had been changing for years. The attraction of tourists that had been the financial backbone in the 1940s and 1950s had slowly shifted.

Instead Long Beach had become a primarily bedroom community for commuters to New York City. The ocean and the beach clubs in Lido and Atlantic Beach were still attracting summer visitors. The boardwalk was still busy with bicyclists, joggers, and walkers, but there were only a few remaining businesses there. The once grand hotels along the ocean, like the Nassau Hotel (where many well-known people stayed and strolled along the boardwalk in formal attire), had become rundown. They were being used for temporary housing for welfare recipients and the elderly. Government agencies were also using the hotels and abandoned summer rentals to warehouse patients who were released from larger mental hospitals, like Creedmoor and Pilgrim State. They were supposed to be cared for in small-scale community centers. There was a serious problem in that people who were running the switch-boards were also dispensing medications—unqualified staff that had no oversight.

Furthermore, we had what we called "walkers," people who wandered the streets barefoot in the winter, not knowing where they were. Being a former police officer, this was a concern to me as we needed to protect the health and safety of these walkers, who would just drift and wind up on people's property, urinating and panhandling. It was a tragic situation.

The Long Beach City Council then passed an ordinance requiring patients to take their prescribed medication as a condition for living there. But the New York Civil Liberties Union immediately challenged the ordinance as being unconstitutional and won. Helping to change the state's regulations on adult-care facilities was Hannah Komanoff, the first woman elected as Long Beach supervisor and the first woman to represent Long Beach on the Nassau County Board of Supervisors (a post she held for three terms, from 1974 to 1985). The new regulations set staffing requirements and outlined medication procedures.

There were also a disproportionate number of people on public assistance who were living in Long Beach. There were numerous building fires—it was believed that many were started by tenants or landlords looking for insurance payouts—and many storefronts and buildings along Park Avenue had seen better days. A dysfunctional government didn't help. It left the city in such poor fiscal shape that it was on the brink of bankruptcy in the 1970s.

There were other concerns contributing to the decline of my beautiful city, like infrastructure issues, problems with road conditions, and high taxes. Eventually I just got tired of asking the City Council and others in control to do things. I figured the best way to get things done was to do it myself.

Geographically within the Town of Hempstead in Nassau County, Long Beach is politically independent and self-governing. The governing body consists of a five-member City Council elected every two years, which appoints a City Manager. Long Beach also elects a Legislator every four years to represent the city on the six-member Nassau County legislative body. At the time our population was thirty-five thousand people during the year, except during the summer when we swelled to eighty-five thousand. These days that summer population can climb to over one-hundred thousand.

The City Council race in 1974 was as an opportunity for me to address the issues that concerned me as a life-long resident of Long Beach. I wanted to hold the line on taxes, and I hoped to upgrade the city's sanitation, police, and fire services. My goal was to attract new residents to Long Beach, in part by developing resources for better income-producing means in the areas of business and recreation.

I ran as an independent Democrat. There were six candidates in the primary. I went to the Board of Elections who had to draw balls out of a kind of container, and you had to pick numbers for the ballot position. I had someone from the Democratic party pick for me, thinking that would be smart. All I had to do was not come in last. Well, I did come in last and lost the primary, which was sort of shocking, because everyone thought I was going to win. But when people vote the row, they have to choose five.

I ran again the following year, reminding people that I had been a Long Beach police officer, and was currently president of the Police Benevolent Association. Campaign materials also told voters I had been Supervisor of Recreation, was past president of the Booster Club and the Swim Club, and that I was a member of the Elks. By then I had also been recognized for my leadership by the Lions, Kiwanis, and Jewish War Veterans.

Even so, 1975 was a contentious primary because Democrats were fighting against Democrats for party leadership. I led the ticket and with Bill Miller, Robert Leslie, Stephen Sabbeth, and Roy Erickson ran against the Republicans, telling voters to "Vote Row A the Democratic Way." Our slogan was, "We are running to make Long Beach a better place." This time I was the top vote getter in an entirely Democratic sweep of the elections. I was sworn in January 1976. Because of a new city charter arrangement, Miller and I, as the two top vote getters, were elected for four-year terms. The others would be up for reelection in 1977.

But we still needed to determine who would be the president of the new, all-Democratic City Council. Traditionally that was whoever led the ticket, which in this case would have been me. My friend, Jerry

Fleischman, who was my attorney, ended up being the Democratic leader, and later became a judge in Nassau County. His whole life has been dedicated to public service in Long Beach. He arranged a compromise with the other Council members, Leslie, Miller, and Sabbeth, that a 3 to 2 vote gave the latter the role of president. As part of the deal, they wanted to oust the Police Commissioner, Ed Buscemi, which I didn't agree with. I had voted with Erickson against Sabbeth, because at the age of twenty-eight he was the youngest City Councilman in the history of Long Beach. I did not think Sabbeth was the most qualified for the job. The three council members who constituted the majority also named Laurence Farbstein as the new City Manager.

My days participating in the life of Long Beach weren't all about politics that year. I also coached in the Long Beach Recreation Department's sports leagues, as well as continued as a lifeguard. By that point I had been lifeguarding since 1957, and had been a Chief Lifeguard Examiner for the City of Long Beach since 1967, acting for the Nassau County Department of Health.

In February1977, I was named the City Council President by a unanimous vote when Steve Sabbeth announced he was resigning the following month due to personal and political reasons.

Controversy and Another Election

We continued to address issues of skyrocketing taxes, an eroding business district, and aging architecture. We also focused on the influx of de-institutionalized mental patients and welfare recipients, as they were referred to in those days. Further, I wanted to concentrate on taking advantage of our ocean location to increase revenue. The $1.5 million community Federal government development funds we received from the U.S. Department of Housing and Urban Development (HUD) didn't quite cover expenses like demolition of structures that were becoming a dangerous nuisance, like the many burned out buildings on Park Avenue. Many of those projects were strangled by bureaucratic legal and contractor issues.

There were also arguments from residents about the cost of their water bills, and many were refusing to pay their water and sewer bills. Two residents, Francis Smith and Francis Hodson, became known as the "'water ladies," because they tried to shut down a Council meeting over this—in fact they consistently became obstructionists over the next few years. All this was happening while we were dealing with a $16 million budget.

We had a lot of controversy like that back then, as we have now. One issue was that the City Council appointed a City Manager, but because this person changed after every election, there was little consistency. The position had become a political football. I thought instead we should have an elected mayor, rather than an appointed person, because there would be more accountability. Ed Grilli, news director at Nassau Radio Corp., sent the Council a letter of agreement, stating, "Having a Mayor elected by the people, instead of a City Manager appointed to the job, makes the administrator answerable to the people. . . not the City Council." It didn't pass, but Edward Eaton, who worked at the city's water treatment plant, became City Manager. In fact, he was appointed two more times after that to serve for twenty-five years. Politics intercedes in what's best for the city, and sometimes politics becomes a priority rather than what is best. Eaton was best for the city and together we worked to turn the city around.

There was also controversy over the fate of the "Superblock." The six-acre parcel, between Riverside and Long Beach Boulevards, East Broadway, and the boardwalk, was originally divided into thirteen separate lots held by a variety of owners. I wanted Long Beach to focus on recreation. They did away with our municipal pool on Magnolia, and I thought this site could be a recreation site for concerts. To this day there are still people who want to develop it, yet it remains locked in controversy about variances and permits for apartments even as I write this. There was also a controversy at that time over a proposed seventeen-story high rise, which was eventually reduced to ten stories. Right now, in 2018, developers are trying to get fifteen-story buildings, when we're only zoned for eight. It has always been contentious to try to get an agreement between all parties to develop what would be best for the city.

In the late 1970s there was talk of bringing in casino gambling on that infamous block, which I originally supported as a means to increase city revenue. In December 1977, a twelve-member Senate Committee on Casino Gambling held an all-day session at City Hall to determine if they should recommend legalized gambling. We were one of five sites being considered. We invited people from Atlantic City to meet with us, and they arrived in the Bay on their yacht. After they left, two days later they were all arrested, so I changed my opinion right away. In New Jersey where the casinos were located was wonderful, but the housing around it wasn't. I didn't want that to happen here.

In 1979, I requested a feasibility study, which we called the Ocean-front Feasibility Plan, to determine the impact of all this development along our beaches. We needed to know what was best for our residents; clearly not dilapidated hotels and vacant land. If there was to be development, whether it was of high-rises, town houses, or recreational facilities, I wanted it to be done the right way, with a study, rather than to be based on opinions, so we could validate whatever actions we took. This was about rezoning the beachfront from Maple Boulevard to New York Boulevard.

During those days there were real concerns about crime. Residents were pushing for an evening curfew on the beach. They wanted an eight o'clock curfew, but I advocated for a curfew of eleven o'clock because I still believe that our beach and boardwalk are our most beautiful assets. If they weren't open in the evening, I felt we would no longer be who we are. We'd just be the "City of Long." Even so, around this time, our home was burglarized, and jewelry was stolen. The police concluded that clues led to the involvement of teenagers. Also, one morning I found a strip of gauze extending out from the gas tank of my station wagon burned right up to the tank. I guess it had gone out before the car blew up. Talk about my work hitting home.

I also contributed toward settling a strike of the Volunteer Fire Department and led the fight to save the City's Recreation Department from proposed budget cuts.

In the summer of 1979, I was engaged in another election as I was seeking a second term. It was a crazy election starting with the primaries, during which there was a newspaper headline in a 1979 issue of the *Independent Voice* that read "Dead Woman Wins an Election." She had passed away two weeks before, which was too late to withdraw her name. Also, the so-called "water ladies," Francis Smith and Francis Hodson, now Councilwomen, supported Murray Pell, to win a place on the November ballot. Pell's election would have given them a majority vote on the Council.

But we also had some fun. In October, we held the first-ever, five-mile City Manager's run, which started and ended on the boardwalk between National and Edwards Boulevards. There were close to five hundred entrants, including men, women, and children, with over four hundred finishers. I was the official starter—and Ellen ran and finished it. The race still takes place annually in Long Beach.

When it came to the City Council race, however, things were still complicated. I favored the development of the shorefront to attract new business and families to the community, and enhancing our recreation. To this day I believe that Long Beach is about recreation. I also supported the selection of professionals for city offices and a coalition between the regular Republican and Democratic organizations. I did not want Pell to win. So I decided to work with Democrat Roy Tepper to put together an independent coalition that included Bruce Bergman, a Republican. I even had fortune cookies made—and I apologize in advance for something that I wouldn't say today—that read, "Wise man say to Long Beach, Vote Weisenberg, Tepper and Bergman, Two from column A and one from Column B." We were the Independent Coalition to Save Long Beach slate. We won, with me leading the votes, so that Tepper and I won four-year terms and Bergman won a two-year term. I became City Council President for the second time.

One of the first things we did was vote to abolish the Zoning Board so we could create a new one. No new buildings had been constructed along the shoreline since 1973. But zoning laws in the 1960s had been bent to allow permitted builders to put numerous high-rises along oceanfront property. Under the new proposal, the area would be converted to a resident/business zone in which either condominiums up to ten stories or one-hundred-foot-high complexes could be constructed in one area, while the rest would be restricted to residential.

One of the first things we did was to go after substandard housing and force "slumlords" to pay property taxes that they owed. The city threatened to seize their properties if they didn't pay up. Within a year, the city collected $1.5 million in back taxes and seized eighty properties. Among them were some properties on the Superblock, like the Buckingham and Commodore hotels, which had been built in the 1940s, but had become rundown apartment houses.

I wrote to the Metropolitan Transportation Authority President Richard Ravitch to bring in extra police protection to the Long Island Rail Road station. The problem was that we had our own law enforcement patrolling the area and dealing with aided cases like medical emergencies. We wanted more officers for prevention, but we didn't get them.

In March 1980, we voted to approve a proposal for a Waldbaum's supermarket to be part of a $5 million, 80,900 square-foot shopping center in the hub of the city's business district. The project depended on the approval of a $1.25 million grant from HUD. So it's not surprising that we had some fairly prominent White House politicians visit our city that month—in part because it was the U.S. Presidential primary season.

First HUD Secretary, Moon Landrieu, toured the West End Youth Center with me and City Manager Edward Eaton. This was one of the sites that HUD was helping to fund. Shortly after, Vice President Walter Mondale came out as well, and met with me, Eaton, Roy Tepper, and Glen Spiritis, who was our Director of Planning and Development, and Franklin Ornstein, who helped develop the REBUILD organization in Long Beach. REBUILD would buy properties for a dollar, fix them up, and sell them for a reasonable price. Together, we toured the West End Youth Center, the North Park Avenue area, and a few other blocks in the center of the city that were all slated to be revitalized with HUD funds.

On April 3, Joseph Kennedy, son of the late Senator Robert F. Kennedy, and nephew to Presidential hopeful Edward M. Kennedy, also visited Long Beach on his uncle's behalf. He attended the Long Beach Democratic dinner dance with me and Ellen in attendance.

Speaking of famous visitors, in 1965 the Rev. Dr. Martin Luther King Jr., visited Long Beach, touring the North Park neighborhood and watching the installation of a roof on the Christian Light Missionary Baptist Church. So it was fitting that when the local pastor, Reverend Jesse James Evans, and other prominent local African-American leaders like NAACP President Wayne Vann, approached the City Council for a place for the city's youth, we supported it. On April 17, we had the official ground-breaking of the North Park Neighborhood Facility Center, better known as the Martin Luther King Center, on Riverside Boulevard. It offers after-school, summer camp, and other programs to this day. By the way, that intersection, East Pine Street and Riverside Boulevard, was renamed MLK Way in January 2018.

But even with all the attention from outside politicians, it wasn't clear that we were going to get that much-needed HUD grant. In fact, we had been told the Urban Development Action Grant (UDAG) was only a remote possibility given that Federal funds were limited that year. When in October 1980, President Jimmy Carter spoke at Hofstra University in one of his town-meeting campaign appearances as part of his Presidential reelection bid, I attended as the President of the City Council. I used to run with a former student from East Meadow who had become a Secret Service agent. I recognized him on the President's detail. He asked if I would like to speak with Carter, and of course, I said yes. I went into the auditorium and there were thousands of people there. A young woman asked, "Who would like to speak with President Carter?" As thousands of hands went up, I was selected.

I took this opportunity to thank President Carter for his desire to help our communities to enhance their business districts, especially a city like ours, which is on the ocean. I told him this Federal grant would give us a real opportunity to develop our business district. Three days later, the call came in. The grant was approved. In fact, it was a $2.3 million grant, the largest in the city's history at the time, making the $10 million (the cost had doubled by that time), 80,900 square foot shopping center in the heart of the city's shopping district a reality. More than $7.6 million in private funds had been committed for the project contingent upon the UDAG fund. It was a milestone step for our city.

Signs of progress were everywhere. In addition to the MLK Center, we broke ground in April for the new West End Firehouse. We met with Long Island Rail Road representatives to ask them to rehabilitate and refurbish the railroad station, and many other construction plans were in the works, like a new two-story home on West Chester Street, a new senior center, and public works projects.

We also organized the Long Beach Youth Olympics with School Board Trustee Scott Abramson. Nearly every city organization participated, from the Lions and Elks to the Police Department. That May, thousands of Long Beach students from kindergarten through high school participated in three days of events, including track and field, gymnastics, bowling, swimming, and running. The biggest event was the Ten Mile Trophy Run. It was a huge success and has been repeated every year since 1976.

The year 1980 was the beginning of what would become the revitalization of Long Beach, that which had been my original goal in getting involved in city politics in the first place. But personally that's when I was working seven days and six nights as a teacher and in recreation on the weekends. It was a busy time of my life, and so any time that Ellen and I were able to be together, she'd be sure to join me. When I coached young athletes, Ellen sat on the sidelines, and the referees and teams just expected her to be there. We attended every function together. Ellen and I were known as one person.

Issues of Race and Controversy

The progress we were making didn't wipe away the occasional racial tensions that existed in Long Beach. We are an integrated community, and incidents between people of color and white people have been occurring as long as our city has been diverse. I go way back with Reverend Jesse James Evans, who was Pastor at the Christian Light Missionary Baptist Church starting in 1966 when it opened. I attended service there on special occasions, and that relationship gave me insight and understanding of the needs of our diverse population.

When I was Recreation Supervisor of Long Beach in the 1960s, we tried to integrate the sports teams, but the black kids didn't want to and that created problems. We were trying to give kids success in their athletic experiences. Being a coach, I know how important it is to work together, and the color of your skin was never in the evaluation; it was the person's ability that mattered. Everybody is entitled to have opportunities and to be treated with respect, and Long Beach has always worked to achieve this. Many of the teams I coached in CYO ended up going to the Catholic schools. We had many talented athletes who participated in Long Beach, kids of all races.

But on June 23, 1980, the racial tensions in Long Beach boiled over in a fight between three hundred black and white youths. The fighting began after several members of the high school's white softball team chased two young black male students, alleging they had initiated fights at the high school that April. There were two other racially-motivated incidents that June as well, one involving a white man who alleged he was attacked by several black youths, and another in which a white man allegedly pointed a shot gun at several people in a predominantly African-American neighborhood.

The Council called in the Nassau County Human Rights Commission. At the meeting, Long Beach Councilwoman Frances Smith said that the outburst was "racially orientated" because the City's one-hundred twenty summer jobs did not go to blacks but to employees who are politically appointed. I explained that three hundred seventy-four young people had been hired for the summer, and that each child was serviced through the Youth Bureau. Of these, one-hundred seventy-six were black, one-hundred sixty-two were white, and thirty-six were Hispanic. I commented at the time: "Smith's statement was erroneous and inflammatory. This is a good community that does work together, and the disturbances in the high school in April and two years ago, as well as last week's trouble, were started by just a few."

There have been other racial incidents between youth since that year, and that is the product of a much larger national issue. But for me, the relationships I have had through coaching young athletes continue to be where I see the most hope for easing these concerns.

Some of the young people who have stood out to me include Sherman Brown. As a high school student, he was an outstanding athlete; champion wrestler, exceptional football player, and all-around wonderful young man. He graduated Long Beach High School in 1970. I saw his potential to achieve anything he worked for. He once asked me if he could have a job in the Sanitation Department. I said, "Sherman, I'd like you to become a lifeguard." He successfully passed the test, becoming the first person of color to work as a lifeguard in Long Beach. He became a member of the Long Beach Lifeguard Patrol and the Lifeguard Tournament team. He also was an active athlete at the MLK and Recreation Centers, and worked as a code enforcement officer for the City's Building Department. He was loved and respected by all who knew him and was a role model for all young people.

We loved Sherman like a member of our family. He and my boys were the best of friends. He played football and weighed two hundred pounds without an ounce of fat. He wrestled one-hundred sixty-seven or thereabouts, but cutting weight is a tremendous strain on one's body. In 1982, he died while coaching a basketball game at the MLK Center. He was only twenty-nine.

All these years later, Sherman Brown's aunt, Fannie, is taking care of Ricky in his group home. How small this world is.

Another wonderful young man I came to know was Charlie Hassell, the only person of color in Long Beach High school in the 1950s. He was in school with me, but he was younger. Like me, he was elected

Mr. GO (General Organization), the most popular student in the school, which was an honor back then. He was a wonderful athlete, loved our recreation program, and actively participated and even worked at Long Beach Recreation. He was a skinny kid with a great heart. He was also a member of the Long Beach team that fought in the Golden Gloves. He lost, but was a champion to all of us here in Long Beach. Charlie passed away a couple of years ago. His cousin Dawntress Hassell was also a great athlete. We trained her to swim and she became a champion in our swim program. She was close to our family.

Leroy Conyers was a Long Beach resident beginning in 1958. He worked for many years for the Recreation Department and Ice Arena. He was also the first director of the MLK Center. He took an active role in our community, and was loved and respected for that. Many thought of him as "the black mayor of Long Beach." He always had a smile and made people laugh. He died in 2000 at age sixty-three.

It's worth noting that in the North Park section of town, a park was dedicated to him; the Leroy Conyers Park at Rev. J.J. Evans Boulevard and Chester Street. It was renovated to include new equipment and a splash park in 2007—and was dedicated to Conyers, as well as Hassell and Brown, for their influence on North Park area residents.

Long Beach Growth and Development

The West End Community Center was an extension built onto West School. It's an interesting story: A man from the Federal government came down to look at West School. We talked in his limousine about running track and my being a state quarter-mile champion. It turned out he was a quarter-miler too, and we commiserated in the limo on how difficult the 440 is. (It's neither a sprint nor a distance race, but something in between and not easy.) I guess I made an impression. Before he even set eyes on the site, he agreed to commit the resources to proceed. The dedication was Saturday, November 8, 1980.

The development of our beloved City attracted everyone's interest, including that of our children. We arranged "Tours of Progress," bus trips around the city over a period of a few months so we could bring attention to what we were accomplishing. Boys and girls from the elementary schools and high school social studies classes were included. The bus tours allowed everyone to see what is being done by their government, to improve their neighborhoods and make Long Beach a better place to grow up in. When I was growing up here, residents always spoke about our city with pride, and I wanted that to happen again.

After a bus tour of the sixth graders from Lindell School, there was an article in the January 4, 1981, Sunday issue of *The New York Times.* The reporter interviewed some of the students and quoted Michael Ward, who was then eleven years old. He wrote a letter to Long Beach City Hall, stating, "If I had one million dollars to spend, I would fix up all the broken-down buildings." Michael also wrote that he'd fix up all the streets with potholes and bumps and cover it all with blacktop.

His classmate, Eddie Dieringer, wrote, "If I'm lucky, I'll have $500 left, and I'll organize a bunch of kids to go around Long Beach with litter bags and pick up garbage for a small salary."

The kids had good ideas, and the Council was taking what they said to heart. Already at that time we were rebuilding and refurbishing much of Park Avenue. We added the tree-lined parking islands. Building facades were reconstructed in the Spanish mission-style with red-tiled roofs and stucco walls. This dovetailed with the style that prevailed in the early 1900s, when Long Beach's development first began in earnest with the arrival of William Reynolds, a thirty-year-old former state senator and real estate developer.

We overhauled the 2.2 mile boardwalk from the beach up at a cost of only $821,000. (Compare that with the $40 million price tag following Superstorm Sandy.) The refurbishment included replacing railings and building a new comfort/lifeguard center, where I spent many hours each summer.

We also eliminated a drainage problem along Laurel Boulevard and reconstructed rundown single-family houses.

We even re-sodded Lindell Field at Long Beach High School, which hadn't been done since 1954, two years after I graduated.

Further, in addition to construction on the West End Neighborhood Community Center and the North Park Neighborhood Facility, both of which I mentioned in earlier pages, we also broke ground on the Senior Citizen Center for our senior population.

As a city government we accomplished a tremendous amount of change in one short year. Roy Tepper, Bruce Bergman, and I were deeply involved with working with the community as well as the agencies, including the Police and Fire Departments, throughout this development program. City Manager Edwin Eaton supported the infusion of Federal aid and kept a close eye on it. The voice of the people was brought to government, working together with the City Council and Eaton. These projects were done in cooperation with the Director of Planning and Development, Glen Spiritis. But there were other projects we were keeping our focus on.

Something else that happened in 1981 was that I was recognized for my twentieth year of service to Long Beach—which also coincided with me being a resident of forty-seven years. I was interviewed by the *Long Beach Journal* to honor the anniversary. I told the reporter that the reason my family and I stayed here is that we love it. I said one of my greatest pleasures is running on the boardwalk—something I enjoy doing to this day. I said, "The view of the ocean and the beach has a calming effect on me and looking at the expanse of sea helps put my life in perspective." I still feel that way. The article ended with me saying, "The people of this community make Long Beach great. The young people, the joggers on the boardwalk, and the bench sitters, the senior citizens, and every resident up and down every street." That's another opinion that hasn't changed for me all these years later.

In 1981, I also received my professional diploma in administration from the Long Island University C.W. Post Campus, which at that time in my career as a teacher was an important step. I saw it as something that allowed me to use my expertise in the area of administration to benefit the Long Beach community in a more professional manner.

Among my many goals on the City Council was emphasizing recreation. Beginning in 1983, the Long Island Marathon ended the grueling twenty-six-mile marathon course on our boardwalk. We also refurbished the Municipal Pier at the Magnolia Boulevard Recreation Center. The fishing pier extended into Reynolds Channel and was a favorite spot to cast a fishing line. In addition, we were rehabilitating the Recreation Center, with roof repairs and an additional steam room. In June that year, the remaining houses on Chester Street were demolished so the beginning of the Waldbaum's Shopping Mall could begin in earnest.

In November 1983, Tepper and I retained our seats for four more years, and City Councilwoman Pearl Weill, who was elected to a two-year term in the 1970s, and again in 1981, received another two-year term. We three incumbents considered this strong showing as an endorsement by the public of the administration's policies. I was then the leading vote getter in three straight elections, so I felt the public was giving us a mandate to continue the progress we began in 1977. At the time, by the way, the annual salary for a Council member was $6,460.

That same month we dedicated a new monument to Long Beach veterans in the center median of Park Avenue at Edwards. It replaced the one that had to be removed to make way for the improved Park Avenue parking malls.

During this period, I was still teaching in East Meadow. In February 1984, the Parents and Teachers Association (PTA) honored my then seventeen years as a special education teacher in the district and my work with the Special Education Parent Teachers Association (SEPTA). I was named "Teacher of the Year." The PTA recognized me for bringing innovative programs into the special education program, like unusual field trips and holiday programs.

In 1984, I received special training in drug and alcohol education from the Nassau County Drug and Alcohol Division. I created a "Kids Against Drugs" program at Meadowbrook Elementary in East Meadow to teach the kids about the dangers of drugs. My special education students presented a play entitled, "A Day in the Life of a Child in an Alcoholic Home." It stressed how alcohol problems can affect family members. I was on the National Council for a Drug-Free America. First Lady Nancy Reagan heard about our program and sent a letter. The First Lady wrote, "Keep up the good work."

The Work Progresses

In August 1984, Long Beach was one of eighty U.S. cities recognized by the Reagan Administration with a National Excellence Award for our successful local community development. The award was presented to the city's Department of Planning and Urban Development, which was still headed by Glen Spiritis.

The development projects in Long Beach continued to keep the City Council members busy. We had a ribbon-cutting ceremony in 1984 to mark the official opening of the Historical Society Offices in the lobby of City Hall.

In 1985, I became assistant principal of East Meadow's Bowling Green Elementary School in Westbury, and spent the next four years in that position. My focus was on our drug-free program and on our special needs students. I was also known to do some crazy things for school spirit like dress up as the Easter Bunny and Ernie from *Sesame Street*.

While there, I instituted another anti-drug program. The slogan was, "The choice for me is drug free." That was around the time a promising young man, Len Bias, who had been drafted by the Boston Celtics, died of a drug overdose. This tragedy drew attention to the problem of drugs among our young people. In many heartbreaking ways, so little has changed today. Our program received quite a bit of attention, and even resulted in a song that was played on Long Island radio stations.

I used to tell the kids: "God has given you the gift of potential. I am here because I love you." The newspapers at the time said that it was this directness of my messages to the kids that was central to my effectiveness. Students participated in essay and poster contests expressing themselves on the issue, winning certificates, savings bonds, and T-shirts with our slogan as rewards.

John Jurick, the U.S. Education Secretary's regional representative, said I had "gone far beyond what is usually seen in elementary schools. The man is living up to a commitment of honor . . . he brings to the school environment a sincerity that is rare indeed. His caring has rubbed off on staff and the net result is an atmosphere wherein students feel special.'"

In the 1988 to 1989 U.S. Education Department's Drug Free School Recognition Program, Bowling Green, was the only Long Island school to be nominated and was one of only seven schools in our state to be so recognized. I was also honored by the Nassau County Department of Health and the Stewart Avenue Association for my drug education program. The key to success is to be involved. The War Against Drugs, like so many of our battles, is one that has to be fought together.

Meanwhile, as Long Beach Council member, with the revitalization of Long Beach now many years in process, I worked to make other improvements with special needs children and adults in mind. In 1987, we had a new ramp installed that led to the fishing pier at Magnolia and the Bay. We got a government grant to obtain a new bus with wheel-chair capabilities. Our goal was to make sure that the city responded to the needs of the physically challenged in every area possible. We also added a handicapped lift at the recreation pool.

But we also took time to introduce other programs, like proclaiming the week of June 3, 1987 as National Safe Boating Week in cooperation with the local Flotilla Chapter of the U.S. Coast Guard Auxiliary. As a water community, it was and still is important that everyone is aware of the rules of the waterway.

In November 1987, I was elected to my fourth, four-year term on the City Council. My platform was that although I was thrilled with the development of Long Beach up to that point, I wanted to improve the city's quality of life. That included expanding public transportation for the elderly, increasing the number of recreation programs, paving roads, improving sewers, focusing on environmental needs, like planting grass in sand dunes along the beachfront to control erosion (which Ellen and I did together), and pushing to stop street corner drug sales. I said that education is the key to fighting drug abuse and that we already had enough police for enforcement.

I attended the White House Conference for a Drug-Free America because, as the *South Shore Tribune* wrote on March 17, 1988, the program I administered at Bowling Green Elementary School was thought of as a "model anti-drug program." At the conference I met Mother Hale who founded Hale House in New York, and who gave homes to the babies of drug-addicted mothers until they were able to care for their children themselves.

In November 1988, the Civic Association of Stewart Avenue in the East Meadow School District gave me a plaque to honor my anti-drug work. The plaque reads: "We deeply appreciate your caring concern for our children and your efforts in teaching them to become drug free." My entire family surprised me by being in attendance that night.

I was quoted thirty years ago in the East Meadow School District's publication, "Steps to Learning," saying about our son, "Ricky . . . helped me to understand how much love special children have to give and how much they can accomplish if we care enough to help them." I feel exactly the same way today.

During those years, I worked with Republican Congressman Jack Wydler and County Executive Francis Purcell, and later, Thomas Gulotta. We had close friendships and mutual respect in achieving the needs of our community. These were really good friends of mine.

I also worked closely with Congressmen Ray McGrath and Peter King, and Senator Alfonse D'Amato, all of whom were Republicans. Senator D'Amato and I have long been friends. Al has always supported our community, and we have worked together many times in the best interests of all. The differences these Republicans and I might have had paled in comparison with the importance of working together for our community.

I worked with Stan Smolkin, an outstanding public servant who served as a Councilman for many years and later as a judge. I coached Kevin Braddish when he was a kid, and then he became a Councilman with me, and then Council President, and later, Democratic chairman.

Jerry Kremer worked as Corporation Counsel for the City of Long Beach and became a State Assemblyman, as well as Chairman of Ways and Means in the State Assembly, where he served for twenty-four years. He worked hard for the people of the State of New York, especially our city. He's a person who surely should be acknowledged in Long Beach for the service he performed in his years in the Assembly.

Bruce Nyman was on the Board of Supervisors, representing Long Beach in Nassau County. Bruce is a smart man, and very creative public relations person who truly loves our city.

My positive interactions with all of these men would later become a solid base on which I would start my career as an Assemblyman.

Those days I served on the City Council were personally busy as my children, Russell, Gregg, Julie, and Vicki each left home and Ricky was at the group home in Melville where we visited him often, and also brought him home to stay. I even became a grandfather. Ellen and I sold the house on Pine Street and bought a condominium on West Broadway with a spare bedroom for Ricky.

In 1986, my mother, Renee Scheckwitz Weisenberg, passed away at age eighty-one after having surgery. I was blessed to have my mother who was born with a heart full of love. She loved everybody in her life. Her values were all about family. She had continued to live in Long Beach, in fact just a few blocks away from us. So Brenda and I, and the rest of the family were always with her, and she came to many of my political events. We were always celebrating life together.

Through all these personal changes a family goes through, I never forgot that my role as a City Councilman was always to focus on what was best for the people of Long Beach—and we learned from them as well. So when an opportunity came along for another way I could make a difference in the lives of children and others in Long Beach—and the state—it seemed a natural fit.

Taking the oath of office in Albany. Ellen accompanied me
whenever I was in Albany serving as assemblyman.

Celebrating diversity of the community on Flag Day in 1997 with students at Lindell School. Danny Lehner, president of the Nassau Council of Chambers of Commerce, provided the flags.

Governor Mario Cuomo signs my bill for soft body armor and automatic weapons for police officers.

Senator Al D'Amato—a supporter of the anti-drug program I initiated at Bowling Green.

Governor George Pataki hands Ellen his pen after he signs a bill to help people and families with disabilities.

Congressman Peter King and I often worked together for the people we served.

Here, I am introducing Father Tom Donohoe to the Assembly in Albany to open the session.

For securing donations to repair and upgrade the Bishop Molloy Recreation Center in Point Lookout, Ellen and I were presented with this plaque in 2008. Father Tom Donohoe (between us) made the presentation.

In 2002, Rabbi Kenneth Hain of Congregation Beth Shalom in Lawrence opens up the session in Albany.

Governor Andrew Cuomo thanks me as he announced ground-breaking legislation to protect people with special needs and disabilities.

HAS YOUR SUNSCREEN EXPIRED?
SAVE YOURSELF !

Check for an expiration date and
PREVENT SKIN CANCER!

**I WILL SAVE YOU
IN ALBANY**

paid for by Assemblyman

**I WILL SAVE YOU
AT THE BEACH**

Harvey Weisenberg

My infamous billboard on Rockaway Turnpike and Brookville Road,
which stayed up from 2001 to 2006. It became known nationally;
people would stop me in airports to ask if I was the guy in the Speedo.

6.

State Assembly, The First Decade

The 20th Assembly district comprises Atlantic Beach, Long Beach, Lido Beach, Island Park, Oceanside, East Rockaway, the Five Towns, and parts of Lynbrook. We were represented from 1966 to 1988 by State Assemblyman Jerry Kremer, a Democrat.

Jerry served as Chair of the Assembly Energy Committee and then moved to the Ways and Means Committee, which he chaired for ten years. In 1986, he was a candidate for Speaker of the New York State Assembly, but Mel Miller, a Democrat from Kings County, was chosen instead. At the beginning of the session of 1987, Miller appointed Saul Weprin, a Democrat from Queens, to replace Jerry as Chair of the Ways and Means Committee. Though Jerry was re-elected to the Assembly in November 1988, he ran for Speaker and was defeated. He resigned on December 14 to pursue business and personal commitments.

His resignation paved the way for a special election to fill his seat, which had been Democratic for twenty-three years. Long Beach Democratic chairman Kevin Braddish wanted to keep the seat in party hands, and though at one point there were eight prospective candidates, Braddish said that he hoped I would win the seat. I was still serving as Long Beach City Councilman. I decided to run because I saw it as a challenge and an opportunity to pursue resources and grants that could be beneficial to the communities of the 20th Assembly district.

In a letter penned January 17, 1989, Jerry Kremer endorsed me to take over his seat, expressing his "belief that you are ready to use your years of local experience to help the people of the 20th Assembly District."

Jerry went on to say, "I hope that all of the members of our party and the voters will join behind you in making sure that this remains a Democratic seat in Albany."

That week I won our party's nomination. The final vote within the Democratic headquarters was Weisenberg, two-hundred seventy-five, Fern Steckler, ninety-nine, John Matthews, forty-seven, and Sam Levine, six.

I was accused by Lawrence Levy, a hard-nosed writer for *Newsday*, of having a fistfight with Democratic chairman Kevin Braddish. Not true. Braddish laughingly pointed out that given our difference in size, the "report was truly comical. My mother never raised me to be a fool." Both of us denied the story in a follow-up article. In fact, Kevin was my campaign director. We remain close to this day.

Levy wrote in a January 23, 1989 editorial, "Long Beach has always been a peculiar place, at least politically. Most of the Jews, Italians, and Irish who moved there from New York still sign on the Democratic line—unlike most people who come to Long Island. . .."

Thus began a three-week campaign against Republican Conservative Charles Kovit. I visited every train depot, supermarket, bakery, and shopping mall in the District with my anti-drug, pro-special education, and environmental improvement campaign. I got endorsements from all the local papers. The *Nassau Herald* said: "Our vote goes to Harvey Weisenberg. We like his style, his individuality. He is refreshingly honest; no airs, no baloney; he tells us what he thinks, like it or not. He is his own man—and he is our man in this special election."

I was elected to the Assembly on Valentine's Day in 1989, and of course, the seat did remain Democratic for the next twenty-seven years. I received a plurality of more than two-to-one in Long Beach, and was sworn in by my friend, then Judge Jerome Fleischman, with Ellen and our children in attendance. I was fifty-five and about to start yet another career. I resigned as assistant principal at Bowling Green, ending my twenty-two-years in East Meadow schools (though it took a while for me to adjust; I called the school every day in those first weeks). In my thirteen years as City Councilman, a position from which I also now had to resign, I was sometimes referred to as Mr. Long Beach. But I was now heading to Albany to work for the state.

My First Year, 1989

After all my years in the City Council, what was immediately different about working in Albany and state politics was that I was impressed by the intelligence and diversity of people who served in the Assembly. If you wanted to get up to speak to everyone, it was clear you had better know what you were talking about. You have to press a button to indicate to the Speaker that you want to speak. You had to be accurate in your presentation because the people were professional, experienced, and knowledgeable. Most of them were lawyers and they knew how to debate the facts.

On my second or third day in Albany, we had a budget meeting at the Governor's mansion with all the Democratic members. Of then Governor Mario Cuomo, Jerry Kremer warned me, "Don't ever cross the Governor. He never forgives or forgets." When Governor Mario Cuomo gave a presentation, everyone, and I mean everyone, was respectfully silent. He could command a room, but it was more than that. It was fear. You're afraid (and more so as a brand new Assemblyman), of saying the wrong thing and bringing his wrath (and long memory) down on you.

When the Governor was talking about Long Island, he referred to us as the "affluent Island," and if there was a need for funding, he suggested that we (Long Islanders) could sell another "polo pony." I patiently waited for someone to say something, but nobody did.

So I did.

"The affluent Island?" I said. "Come to my city and I'll show you our soup kitchen, and people who are living under the boardwalk! Long Beach certainly is not affluent. We have a population of need! And that's why I'm here."

To get the full impact of this, you have to understand the visual. Everyone was standing around Governor Cuomo, and by the time I had finished this speech, everyone had moved away, leaving just myself and Mario standing together. At that point, Assemblyman Saul Weprin ended the budget discussion.

Afterwards, members of the Black and Puerto Rican caucuses asked me if the Governor had invited me to sleep over. Other members came over and suggested that I not start my own car. But before I left the mansion, Governor Cuomo smiled at me. And I said, "I am happy to be here with you."

I learned then that the Governor enjoyed being challenged. For me, what's on my mind is on my tongue. I would respectfully challenge him and give him an opportunity to discuss topics he knew well. I had insight that I think he enjoyed hearing.

The next meeting was to include a vote on the death penalty in New York State, which the Governor was against. As a former police officer, I was in favor of it for criminals who murder peace, police, or corrections officers. They put their lives on the line every day, and we need to afford them some protection.

I knew Mario Cuomo would veto the bill, and he did. I respected his views on the issue and I believe he respected mine. I pushed hard for an override to his veto, which required one-hundred votes. We got ninety-seven. I brought the issue to a vote every year, and Cuomo vetoed it every year.

I also went after the Governor for cutting education budgets. I've advocated for educators, for our children's education, and for special needs programs since I first started teaching in the 1960s. As soon as I joined the State Assembly, I pointed out the need for the Governor and Legislature to be sensitive to the needs of our children, particularly those with special needs. I continued this advocacy throughout my career. It was a cornerstone of my professional life, and at least in the beginning, I was the only one talking about these important issues.

Early in my time in Albany, I advocated for anti-drug education to begin earlier than in high school, when it may, in many cases, be too late. My friend Senator Al D'Amato introduced me to William Bennett, Director of the President's National Drug Control Policy Program, the Federal government's "drug czar." He had expressed an interest in the anti-drug program I had initiated at Bowling Green.

"'Every day on our loudspeaker, when we do morning exercises," I explained, the kids are asked, "What do Bowling Green kids say?" And a thousand kids answer, "The choice for me is drug-free!"

Bennett, who was also the Secretary of Education under President Ronald Reagan, said of my program, "It looks to be one of the very good ones."

I participated in a press conference on the subject in Washington, D.C. in February. Ellen and I flew down to D.C. in one of those little commuter aircrafts, the ones that are the size of a bathroom with flimsy canvas doors. I felt ill during the whole flight and upon landing ran to a bathroom and threw up. Still more than a little green, I walked out of the bathroom and into the lights and cameras of the press conference. All in a day's work.

In October 1989, at a luncheon Bennett attended, he asked me for information on my anti-drug program, indicating that he was going to suggest that similar programs be instituted in schools throughout the nation.

At that luncheon I said, "The reality facing today's educators is that the family, as a core of instruction, is declining in influence among children. Values are being imposed by the street, and the lowest elements in the media. More and more, schools are becoming a place where hot breakfast is served, sex education is being taught, and after-school activities are expanded. More and more, it is encompassing the entire day of the student."

I went on to point out, "We may not like the fact that the role of the family in education is growing weaker . . . but the fact is that it is happening. It becomes important that we prepare our youths to be better educated for living in today's society."

Please understand that in all my jobs, from police officer to teacher to public servant, I have focused, on among other things, the importance of caring for, nurturing, and guiding our youth, because they represent our future.

In March 1989, Ellen and I, along with other legislators, were invited to a luncheon at Gracie Mansion by Mayor Ed Koch. I admired him. He was very personable and we became friends. For this luncheon, Ellen made a cake for dessert. We then received a very nice letter from the Mayor, stating, "Thank you very much for the wonderful homemade coffee crumb cake. It was delicious. Many thanks for your thoughtfulness." Ellen always found a way to add a personal touch to enhance whatever work I was doing.

On March 24, 1989, the Exxon *Valdez* oil spill occurred in Prince William Sound, Alaska. An oil tanker owned by Exxon Shipping Company struck the Bligh Reef, spilling 10.8 million gallons of crude oil over the next few days. That event is now considered to be the second largest oil spill in U.S. waters, after the 2010 Deepwater Horizon spill. It is still known as one of the most devastating human-caused environmental disasters.

In response, in May I organized a one-day boycott of all Exxon products, together with then Assemblymen Tom DiNapoli, a Democrat representing Great Neck, and Maurice Hinchey of Saugerties, who later became a Democratic congressman. The boycott was the result of a bill we co-sponsored, which amended the Environmental Conservation Law to improve oil spill prevention, control, and compensation. Provisions were designed to help prevent future oil spills and to assure action by the guilty parties in the cleanup of future spills.

At about the same time, I introduced legislation to amend the state finance law related to particular state contracts involving biodegradable packages and containers. The idea was to address the shortage of landfill space by reducing the amount of biodegradable packaging disposed of by state agencies.

In April, there was a proposal to cut funds to public education. As a former teacher, I have always been in the corner of educators. As I said at that time, and as I still believe today: "The future of our nation lies in the values and attitudes we instill in today's young people. To cut education is to sacrifice their future."

As a legislator, I was also in a unique position to understand that projects may be championed, even approved, but without mandates for money, they go nowhere. Cuts in education budgets, I explained at that time, made "by a distant bureaucracy, are of limited value since the critical student-teacher relationship is compromised. I have zero tolerance," I was quoted as saying on April 21, 1989, "for cuts that directly affect the classrooms and needs of special students. This is (and remains today) a line from which I will not retreat."

So I lobbied overnight and into the early morning to bring $914,000 in additional aid to the Long Beach School District. The final vote to approve took place just before five-thirty in the morning. We were up all night, but we got it done!

As a former police officer, I was able to understand that the criminal elements were becoming more dangerous and we had to meet the challenge head on. I saw firsthand the desperate need to protect our law enforcement personnel in the war on drugs. I worked with the Senate and my colleagues across the aisle to allow the Cities of Long Beach and Glen Cove to acquire soft body armor and automatic pistols for police officers. "There have been too many instances," I was quoted as saying at the time, "of police officers being killed or maimed while in a gun battle with drug dealers using more advanced pistols with greater fire power."

Governor Mario Cuomo called me at home to congratulate me for bringing this bill, which he had just signed. The call came in on my speaker phone and when the Governor told me who it was, I said, "Stop the crap," and was about to hang up. But Mario convinced me that he was indeed who he claimed to be, and went on to suggest that I introduce a bill to make this help the police statewide. I thanked him for his support, and together we passed legislation to do exactly that. I'm glad I didn't hang up on him.

I joined with then Nassau County Executive Thomas Gulotta, a Republican, to honor the late Jim Conlon, who had been paralyzed by an aneurism in 1968, and Vic Ferrante, co-presidents of Citizens United to Remove Barriers (CURB). Along with Jim Monahan, Conlon started a one-man campaign to bring curb cuts to Long Beach. Two-hundred students at Long Beach Catholic School were inspired by Conlon and CURB and wrote me letters asking me to take legislative action supporting their work. The City of Long Beach got the message, installing curb cuts on every street corner in Long Beach. At the time, Long Beach was the only municipality in the state to install the cuts. CURB has made life easier for many of our residents with physical disabilities, enabling them to get around more easily, and thereby enjoy an increased quality of life. Over the years, Conlon's advocacy ensured that there are ramps, rails, chair lifts, elevators, and scooters available to Long Island residents.

That June, I joined with Police Commissioner Gerard Valle, the PBA leadership, and thousands of citizens who rallied on the steps of the state capitol to override an expected veto by the Governor to allow for the death penalty for criminals who kill police officers. This is a difficult issue, and my position was taken with mixed feelings. The taking of a life is a critical, difficult decision, and an extreme penalty. But to this day I feel it is important to punish those who kill police officers. The Governor did, in fact, veto the measure.

Around that time, the State Legislature had appropriated $500,000 for the establishment of a Nassau-Suffolk Office for a Health Systems Management Agency. It would monitor Long Island's health facilities, including hospitals, nursing homes, and other health care facilities that were currently overseen by an office in New Rochelle. However, I learned at a State Health Department meeting that the money had not yet been released. The money was, in effect, fictional. Appropriated, but not released. In other words, nothing.

So, as I came to be in the habit of doing, and not just with Governor Cuomo, I went right after him, publicly demanding that the money be released. I explained in a local newspaper that for half of Long Island's facilities to be monitored by an office in Westchester certainly warranted more local oversight, and so I demanded it of the Governor and it was released.

Meanwhile I continued to lifeguard, which at that point I had been doing for thirty years. I wasn't about to give up saving lives just because I had another job to do. On the days I didn't need to be in the office, I traded in my three-piece, pin-striped suit for a swimsuit and T-shirt. I was paid $250 a week for my lifeguard services. No one seemed to mind. What better place to meet the people you serve than the beach?

In a July 10, 1989 *Newsday* article about this, another Long Beach lifeguard was quoted saying, "Harvey's what? Fifty-six?" asks lifeguard John Burke, 22. (I was actually still fifty-five, but who's counting?) "And would you believe he swims better than at least half of the lifeguards on this beach?" What would John say if he knew I'm still lifeguarding at age eighty-four?

A related article in the *Nassau Herald* gave me a chance to express what lifeguarding meant to me then, and it's still true today. Besides my love for education, one of the reasons I chose to enter that field was that it gave me an opportunity to be a lifeguard and have my wife and children enjoy the summers with me during those years. At first it was to help look over our children, but later we all worked together. Russell, Gregg, Julie, and Vicki are all certified lifeguards, and Ellen had been a lifeguard in the 1950s working at the Lake Success Village Pool. Over the years, she often worked as a summer nurse for the Long Beach programs.

But my love of the beach was more than a family experience. Referring to becoming a lifeguard at age twenty-five, I said, lifeguarding is one of the most wonderful, educational, and enjoyable experiences a young person can have. A lifeguard is in touch with God's given beauty, the ocean. The ocean is both powerful and awesome. While it presents a beauty, it presents a danger if it is not understood and respected. I never got bored sitting up in the lifeguard chair looking over the ocean.

Every day is different. You learn to acknowledge and respect the birds, the water, and the beach. It puts you in touch with the reality of life.

It also gave me a chance to work with kids, to educate them about the ebb and flow of the tides. I taught many Long Beach children how to swim, quite a few of whom went on to become lifeguards. I said all that in 1989, but my feelings about lifeguarding haven't changed.

It has been a privilege to serve the people in so many ways. As I was quoted in an August 1989 article: "In the summer months, I'm helping to save the lives of persons in the water. In the winter, fall, and spring, on the legislative side, I'm helping to save lives by working for laws against illegal drugs, for improving the lives of senior citizens, public safety, special needs kids, and against the proliferation of crime."

I really did enjoy a positive, sometimes even lighthearted relationship with other public servants, even my colleagues across the aisle. There's a photo that was taken at a Chamber of Commerce meeting at Vito's restaurant in Long Beach of former Republican Assemblyman and County Executive Tom Gulotta at a podium shying away from someone accosting him in a gorilla suit. That was me.

Ellen and I were named honorary chairpersons for the Juvenile Diabetes Research Foundation's (JDRF) Second Annual Walk/Run-a-Thon for October 1989. Because of Ellen's own struggles with type 1 diabetes, the JDRF had been a source of information for her. She volunteered with the organization—which only focuses on research for type 1 diabetes— to provide her professional experience as a nurse. It was also a way for her to keep up-to-date with the latest studies, so our support as a family was ongoing.

In 1989, I spoke out about an issue that has long been important to me, as a Long Beach resident and lifeguard, boating safety and the irresponsibility and sometimes intoxication of repeat offenders. At a public forum in Point Lookout on the issue, I cited statistics from that time that some thirty percent of deaths through boating are caused by intoxicated boaters. "We would not tolerate the existence of such drivers on our roads," I said then. "Why should we do so on our beautiful waterways?"

I recommended legislation and worked with State Senator Norm Levy, a Republican from Merrick who had sponsored the Point Lookout meeting. But as always, real change comes down to funding, and the willingness of our elected officials to provide meaningful financial support for issues that are in the public's interest.

I introduced legislation to limit the use of Jet Skis near bathing areas and other boating environments. I also introduced legislation for "implied consent" for anyone operating a boat if there was evidence they are operating the vessel while impaired by drugs or alcohol, a measure that had already been in effect for automobile drivers. "Implied consent" means that the driver or boat operator consents to sobriety or drug tests simply by having a driver's license or by virtue of being the boat operator.

I have long been particularly sensitive to and occasionally incensed by hate in all forms; bigotry, anti-Semitism, sexism, bullying, and other forms of mistreatment based on a person's background, color, religion, disability, or gender. I wrote a letter in a local newspaper about the ugly scourge of hate that took the form of the defacing of buildings, arson, beatings, even murder, in the vicinity. We have such a wonderfully diverse society. So many different groups contribute such beauty, such art and love in their own unique culturally diverse way.

Where does it begin? I asked that question then, but even today when I ask the same question my answer is the same. In the home. In the street. It may start with an ethnic joke thought by the teller to be harmless. It could start with a perceived economic rivalry, or with ignorance about those who may be different than the people with whom we are familiar. Pointing out this hate to our children and explaining that it is not acceptable is so important. Bigotry does not simply go away. History has proven this time and again. Our beautiful country flourishes because of our diversity.

In the letter, I referred to our society as more than a melting pot: We are "an alliance."

Soon after the letter was published, I spoke at a rally commemorating Kristallnacht with Caryn Katz, director of the Long Island Region of the Anti-Defamation League of B'nai B'rith, which included Dr. Leon Bass, who helped to liberate one of the concentration camps. The rally included a beautiful torchlight procession at the Holocaust Memorial Monument at Long Beach's Kennedy Plaza in front of City Hall.

As an educator, I firmly believe it is vitally important to teach young people to have mutual respect, and to show tolerance of others. In fact, they should learn to celebrate our differences. This is an issue that is very personal to me.

I participated in the Intergroup Community Understanding

Coalition (ICU) formed by my friends at B'nai B'rith, to combat racial, ethnic, and religious bias, this following a spate of ugly incidents of hateful vandalism in, among other places, the Five Towns. I spoke out against the hate speech and disgusting symbols and those who spread them, saying, "I hate to see these little suckers become heroes. We've got to ostracize them."

As my first year in Albany came to a close, I was impressed that through my experience in the Assembly I had learned so much from listening to how others presented their views about the issues. It broadened my understanding of how State politics works, and boosted my ability to bring to view and stress the points needed to be successful in my presentations so I could further achieve legislative success. There were so many good people there who could really debate the issues. It was a learning experience for me on a daily basis.

1990—The Year of Education Funding

I have long fought for funding in education. We have a history of excellence in education here on Long Island. I cited statistics in a 1990 letter to the editor in a local paper: Eighty percent of our teachers at that time had master's degrees; the average in New York State was sixty-five percent. Our students had been high-scoring, award-winners by many measures, but the costs are high when compared to the rest of the state. Funding the education of our kids is a critical part of having a successful, compassionate society, yet it is not always popular.

A systemic problem I saw and spoke out against in the early 1990s is one I still see rampant in our system; our lawmakers' mandated programs go unfunded. Allocating money to budgets to follow through on our promises is part of the road to success, however painful that may be. People are upset about taxes they perceive to be high—and they are high. I noted at the time that young people who are perceived to value education may be thought of as "nerds" and looked down upon. Are you kidding me?

As I said at the time, schools do not operate in a vacuum. They must be supported by our lawmakers, and yes, even our taxpayers. This is part of the price for the high standards we hold for our wonderful country.

You have no idea how contentious a budget fight can be in a legislative body. Everyone believes his or her priorities to be vitally important for their electorate, their people. The allocation or lack of funding is sometimes taken personally. My fight for the funding of our young peoples' education was personal, and I was more than sincere. I was tenacious in my advocacy and in confronting Governor Cuomo on this issue.

We had what was perceived to be a "tax crisis" in early 1990. We called an all-day session at the County Executive's office in Mineola on March 1 to seek positive input from school superintendents, the PTAs, Board of Education members, and other school officials as to how to get our "best bang for the buck."

These are tough problems, folks. Taxes here were and still are high. Yet, we must find ways, sometimes creatively, to address the needs of our young people. And so I reached out for help. Seeking input is part of being a successful representative of our citizens. Everyone's input is valued. This is true democracy at work.

When I found out that the State Senate has proposed legislation in 1990 to curtail aid to homes for the mentally impaired, I heard from the public in the form of letters and calls. I was personally so outraged that I spoke out publicly against the move that would, as I said at the time "pull the funds out from under the most defenseless segment of our population to appease business and industry. . .. A legislator's top priority must be the protection of the less fortunate people, who through no fault of their own must rely on government funding to maintain their quality of life. Mental illness, birth defects, and other disabilities are handicaps which no one chooses to bring upon themselves. If government does nothing else, it must take care of these people. . ."

That politicians would take funding away from those who need it most for political purposes infuriated me—and still does. At the time, the commissioner of the Education Department didn't know anything about special needs education. In fact, at first I had to be the one in the Assembly to educate everyone about the needs of special needs children and to show them why they should care.

In April of that same year, I had my picture taken with actor and environmental activist Alec Baldwin, who was supporting the environmental bond issue that was to appear on the November ballot. *Superman* actor Christopher Reeve was also there.

As a former police officer, I have always supported and fought for our men and women in blue. In 1990, I brought a resolution to establish May 15 as Police Memorial Day, a day set aside to recognize the sacrifices made by our police officers and to pray for their safety. It took until 1997 for this to come to fruition, but this was the beginning of the research.

That was a good year, as I was able to secure nearly $14 million in state aid and pension payment reductions for the City of Long Beach and our local school districts. I recommended that the City and School District consider utilization of this funding increase for relief of taxpayers. I emphasized at that time that pension systems are overfunded.

I also secured $120,000 in grants for the Long Beach Police Department's Crime Resistance Patrol Unit; $20,000 for the Advocacy Committee for Senior Citizens; a $15,000 grant for the Beach YM-YWHA; a $10,000 grant for Circulo de la Hispanidad for its Project SALVA; and $10,000 for the Long Beach Advancement for the Arts organization to develop a community band. I also secured a $10,000 grant for the Parkinson's Support Group Foundation of Long Island, along with a $10,000 award to the ambulance service of Long Beach Hospital.

On a local level, I worked with Long Beach Council President Kevin Braddish and Supervisor Bruce Nyman to add a measure of safety to the canals area. Residents had been expressing concern about the speed of vehicles passing through this high-density residential neighborhood. The bridges spanning the canals had been built too high for drivers to see traffic on the other side of the bridge, which was dangerous. We introduced and passed a fifteen-mile per hour speed limit. I was also instrumental in passing similar speeding restriction laws in Point Lookout and the president streets.

I was on the Transportation Committee in the State Assembly for twenty-five years, and brought a bill in 1990 requiring that every child who is a passenger on a school bus have a seat.

In July 1990, I was "lauded," in the words of one newspaper, by Mario Cuomo, who visited Long Beach and, at the King David Manor presented the city with a check for over $500,000 to battle beach erosion.

Water safety legislation I had brought in 1989 regarding Jet Skis made its way to Governor Cuomo for approval. The number of accidents involving Jet Skis, referred to as "personal watercraft," essentially had quadrupled from 1983 to 1988, and the number of injuries resulting from those accidents also rose dramatically. Requirements of the bill included: Anyone riding on or being towed behind a Jet Ski must wear a life jacket. Anyone riding on a jet ski must wear a cut-off switch attached to his or her life jacket, clothing, or body. No one may lease, hire, or rent a Jet Ski to anyone under sixteen years of age. No Jet Ski may be operated within five hundred feet of a designated bathing area. Jet Skis may only be operated during the period of time one half hour before sunrise and one half hour after sunset.

Being a lifeguard charged with keeping bathers safe and seeing a motorized vessel heading into a bathing area was a frightening sight. These vessels and bathers do not mix; they do not belong in any designated bathing area. Our bill increased the safety of bathers, boaters, and the Jet Ski operators themselves.

This was July 1990, little more than halfway through my first year in the Assembly. I am so proud to have been part of such positive change in so short a time. My work in the State Assembly was just getting started!

In August 1990, I met with Federal Aviation officials and community leaders, along with Congressman Ray McGrath, to discuss excessive noise from jet planes over the Five Towns. As I said at the time, "You really must have a Long Island mentality to understand what the problems are."

Also that year, Nassau County claimed an exemption to the Freedom of Information Act (FOIA), and I fought successfully against the exemption, and for the public's right to know. I have always had to balance my longstanding support of the police with the right of the public to transparency. I sponsored a bill, signed by Governor Cuomo later that summer, to repeal the exemption of the Nassau County's Probation Office, Police Department, Attorney's Office, and District Attorney's Office FOIA regulations, a measure that was not without controversy. I support the great work of those offices, but as I was quoted at that time, "It was ridiculous to think you can close off government records from the public."

On Sunday August 26, 1990, *The New York Times* generously gave me the opportunity to reflect on the many qualities, requirements, skills, loves, and ultimately, the stewardship of being a lifeguard. Because of my decades of lifeguarding, I was in a unique position to tell the public, in this most public and respected of forums, about the lifeguard's dedication to his or her own peak physical condition, love of the ocean and beach environment, understanding of wind, tides and rip currents, and respect for the awesome power of the sea. Rather than battle the ocean, we must travel through it so as not to exhaust ourselves in the critical efforts to save others. I have had the opportunity and obligation to save lives, and to protect nature in this city I love so much—deeply satisfying pursuits.

Just over a month after the article was published, New York State gave $500,000 to the Long Beach Barrier Island for a survey to stave off coastal erosion. I love our beach and am grateful to have the opportunity to protect it.

Because I had won a special election for Jerry Kremer's seat, I had to run for re-election for a full two-year term in November 1990. I was running against Republican Conservative Maura Christ and Right-to-Life candidate Raymond Solga. So much of politics is about campaigning for the next run and the newspapers had their say about me. Mostly it was favorable, that I had been a quick study and accomplished a lot in my term. I had earned a high eighty-two percent favorable rating from the nonpartisan Environmental Planning Lobby, which tracks legislators' environmental votes.

But *The New York Times* said: "Weisenberg has earned a reputation as being confrontational. He interrupted one of Gov. Mario Cuomo's speeches in the Governor's Mansion one day to argue that state education aid to Long Beach should not be cut because Long Islanders are overburdened by taxes. He will call department commissioners at the drop of a hat and ask for money for a drug rehabilitation program or try to bring a constituent's complaint to their attention." Guilty as charged—and I continue to use this approach to this day.

I won my first full term with sixty-one percent of the vote.

1991—Sludge

In early 1991, the Nassau County Board of Supervisors had cleared the way for the building of two giant sludge processing pelletization plants in Cedar Creek, Wantagh, and Bay Park, East Rockaway, at a cost of $140 million. I was aware of illnesses resulting from the harmful emissions from landfills and other treatment plants, and proposed Department of Environmental Conservation guidelines to protect the health and well-being of people who live near facilities such as these.

There was pressure to go ahead with these projects, which were additions to existing facilities. But upon further investigation, I found that pelletization plants similar to those proposed had incidents of dangerous fires, and in the case of Tampa, Florida, a small explosion. At the time, this was a new process, with potentially toxic emissions going into the air, which is why existing projects included hundred-foot smoke stacks. The potential for health hazards in our children or grandchildren years, or even decades, down the line was just too important for me to ignore. Fire hazards and the eighteen-wheelers that would truck tons of the pellet residue past schools on local roads were sources of great concern, requiring further study, before projects such as these could be undertaken.

Nearly a year later, in 1992, a federal judge ruled to allow the county to extend its deadline on awarding the contract. So I worked together with Mayor Irving Shaw of East Rockaway to ask that County Executive Gulotta expedite the process.

As a member of the Assembly Transportation Committee, I sponsored legislation in 1991 to rebuild Park Avenue between Laurelton and Lafayette Boulevards. Local officials claimed that there was no funding to pay for such repairs, so it was up to me to fund the repairs, not only of this section of Park Avenue, but for the whole length of the street, via the State budget. I was able to garner one million dollars from the New York State Department of Transportation's Marchiselli program for the work.

I have always worked hard to strengthen and safeguard the rights of people with disabilities. When families were first referred for evaluation, a bill I brought, and which Governor Mario Cuomo signed into law, stipulated that parents of handicapped children must receive a booklet about special education services. "A Parent's Guide to Special Education Services," a bilingual booklet from State Education, spelled their rights regarding evaluation and placement of their child in programs.

In the fall of 1991, I was drafted by the Democratic Party to be on the Nassau County Board of Assessors, a position I not only had no interest in, but had said I would resign from if elected. Nassau was—and still is—a Republican county. I had been drafted to run for this position because, as a popular candidate whose name was associated with positive causes, my name on the ticket would help the other Democratic candidates on that row on the ballot. I actually defeated incumbent Abe Seldin on the Democratic versus Republican lines, but lost by a slim margin because of the Conservative line vote. The week after the election, the Democratic Party ran an ad in the newspaper thanking me for helping to carry them to victory. Apparently all Democratic candidates made tremendous gains and cut deeply into Republican numbers, according to a newspaper article at that time, because of my presence on the ballot.

1992—Evacuation Plans

I found it incredulous that taxpayers in small cities such as Long Beach did not have the right or ability to vote on school budgets, so I did something about it. In early 1992, I introduced a bill that gave taxpayers the ability to vote on the school budgets they are paying for, and also added provisions for contingency budgets, including expenses for legal obligations, expenses to maintain existing educational services, and expenses to preserve the property of the district. About time!

Two bills I was especially proud of in 1992 lowered taxes for home and condo owners. The first was on behalf of owners of two adjacent lots who, until that time, were exorbitantly taxed, as though one were a commercial property. The other law prevented condo and co-op owners from having to apply and pay for certificates of occupancy (COs) for their individual units. Unit owners had been under the impression that they were in full compliance, and with my help, now they are.

If you can believe it, controversy swirled about there being a cohesive evacuation plan for Long Island. The issue came to view following the devastation wreaked on Louisiana and Florida by Hurricane Andrew in August 1992. The pushback was on the part of fifteen Nassau County school districts that refused to allow their facilities to be used as emergency evacuation shelters. I organized a meeting, held at the end of October 1992 at the Town of Hempstead's Conservation and Waterways building in Lido Beach, with Long Beach City Manager Ed Eaton, Atlantic Beach Mayor Earliene Shipper, officials from the Point Lookout-Lido Beach Fire Department, and then Inspector John Blackenhom, head of the Nassau County Office of Civil Preparedness.

A meeting the previous week, on October 23, had grown heated when Blackenhorn accused barrier island officials of failing to cooperate with the county in preparing for a storm. When pressed on the issue, Blackenhorn admitted that the plan he had alluded to did not actually exist. Cooler heads prevailed, and all parties agreed to work together on an evacuation plan, should a serious storm ever hit our barrier island. As we have seen since, working together in the face of nature's awesome power, before, during, and after storms, is crucial to our survival as a barrier island.

In the election year 1992 I won my second term. Someone once asked me what the State Assembly was like. My answer? It's like a melting pot, because this esteemed body of humanity is here as representative of all people who reside in the state of New York. This really is true. We have such diversity. We have liberals, conservatives, Democrats, Republicans, downstate representatives, upstate representatives, and people from New York City. Each represents constituents with valid needs and concerns, but the constituencies are different and not always in sync. Yet we have to come together as a body, and legislate, addressing the needs of each, and of the state as a whole. Budgets are, by nature, finite. We have to meet the needs of all, as best we can, with whatever funds are available in the budget each year.

New York City has greater representation than Western New York and Long Island. Therefore, my work was cut out for me. I had to advocate for the needs of our people, the folks I represent, who pay high utility bills, and such high taxes. My sometimes volatile relationship with Mario Cuomo and the disparate interests of my fellow Assembly members took a backseat to all of us, both sides of the aisle, coming together to work for the benefit of all with whatever funds were at hand. Imperfectly, yes, but we did this, and it was usually done with respect and courtesy. Oh how government has changed!

I was here for the big one, the horrific hurricane and one-hundred-year flood in September 1938. I lived in the Broadway apartments at the time and I remember looking out the window and seeing someone's roof floating down the street. It was devastating. I also remember the northeaster of December 1992, during a full moon and eclipse, which also brought awful flooding.

1993—Planning for Future Storms

I was realistic and deeply concerned. I felt we desperately needed an emergency plan should there be another natural disaster, so in February 1993, I was made chairman of the New York State Assembly's new subcommittee for the Protection of Long Island's Barrier Beaches. Our panel, which included Atlantic Beach Mayor Shipper and my good friend and environmental activist, Morris Kramer, would hold hearings about evacuation in the face of severe hurricanes. We reached out to fire departments, police, rescue squads, the Red Cross, and our hospitals and gathered real information.

At that time there was simply no evacuation plan in place. I pointed out that the 240,000 people who lived south of Sunrise Highway could not be moved to safety in the face of a category-three hurricane, and the lives of tens of thousands of barrier island residents, not to mention their property, would be at risk.

I advocated to have signs put up, indicating evacuation routes. When that didn't go anywhere, I asked the Governor, "Why not have some of the residents of our jails make the signs?" The signs got made. When the next hundred-year storm, Superstorm Sandy, battered our barrier island in 2014, evacuation signs were valuable aids for the multitudes of people rushing to safety.

Following that December 1992 northeaster, I worked with Hempstead Town Presiding Supervisor Joe Mondello to bring in tons of concrete and stone for use in slowing beach erosion in Point Lookout. It was vital to ensure that no storm would isolate that beautiful village from the Meadowbrook Parkway. While this was great, it was a stopgap measure. A much bigger project, with comprehensive funding, would eventually follow. But acknowledging the problem, and addressing it with that initial tons of concrete and stone from the New York State Department of Transportation, was a great and important beginning.

We had a series of comprehensive hearings. The 1992 northeaster had caused outages and fires in our evacuation center, Long Beach Hospital. It was a real wake-up call, and I wasn't going to let the impact of that shot across the bow to pass without action to protect our barrier island and residents.

Our efforts and advocacy were rewarded when $1.2 million in state funds were awarded to the eastern end of our barrier island for the restoration of beaches and facilities that had been devastated by December's storm and a severe blizzard in March. It was an issue that would remain a priority throughout my career. To this day, I see the ocean creeping halfway up the beach during some full moons.

In May 1993, I was honored by the Nassau County Police Conference as their Man of the Year. Also that May, I spoke out about protecting our barrier island from coastal erosion prior to the fast approaching storm season. The Army Corps of Engineers had conducted studies, but I wanted more. "No more studies!" I said to state officials. "I'm telling you to go a little bit further and a little bit higher."

Meanwhile, multi-billion dollar storm-related payouts by the insurance industry following Hurricane Andrew, a category 5 Atlantic hurricane that struck the Bahamas and Florida in mid-August 1992, as well as other natural disasters, led to some major carriers threatening to scale back coverage. In some cases they refused coverage for properties near the water. So I met with some of these carriers to see what could be done about it.

When I learned that insurance companies decided to discontinue issuing new personal property insurance—both fire and homeowners—and possibly not renewing policies for existing customers in coastal areas, I spoke out in a July 1993 letter to the editor. I wrote: "I do not believe that insurance companies paid out excessive amounts in our region last year. Secondly, they are taking these drastic measures based not on fact, but on potential: the potential that this year's storm season could bring greater devastation. But isn't that why we all buy insurance in the first place? Isn't that why homeowners pay premiums year after year after year? We buy insurance because we know that in life there is always a potential for disaster and we take the steps we can to protect our homes, property, and families. It is simply not justifiable to deny insurance coverage to the residents of the Long Island barrier beaches because of a 'potential.' Insurance companies are there to make a profit," I wrote, "but they are also there to serve the public."

I also attended a meeting on coastal damage on Fire Island where speakers complained about the delays in getting permits for beach replenishments. The co-chairwoman of the state's Coastal Erosion Task Force told an already angry crowd that the task force report would not be available until October. "You're going to have a hard time here," I told her. "The hurricane season began in June . . . The people here can't wait!"

I brought the public together with agency officials and some other public servants, including a FEMA official and the deputy supervisor of the Insurance Department of the State of New York. That supervisor had a hard time speaking, and justifiably so, as the crowd jeered and booed when he repeatedly tried to address them. He suggested that residents take precautions to protect their homes against storms, and insisted that insurance companies were, in fact, continuing to write policies. The crowd would have none of it. When your home is threatened by the awesome power of nature, you get upset and do what you have to do.

I was quoted in *The New York Times,* calling on Governor Mario Cuomo to start a state-level investigation because "companies are redlining Long Island, by saying what could happen, happened somewhere else in the country and so we're not going to insure you. I want to know why they're putting us into a different category from anywhere else in the state of New York."

"What the insurance companies are doing is despicable," my friend Councilman Ed Buscemi said. He was right.

I was also quoted in the *New York Daily News:* "The whole east end of Long Island is uninsurable, according to some of these companies. It's geographical discrimination and it doesn't make any sense."

Another controversial issue I took on involved firearms, specifically negligently stored firearms. Always with heated debate, and despite active opposition by the National Rifle Association (NRA), the Assembly passed my Children's Weapon Accident Prevention Act every year for almost twenty years. The bill would have allowed a gun owner to be charged with a felony if a child under the age of eighteen accessed an unlocked and loaded firearm and injured someone with it. If someone were killed as a result of a gun owner's negligence, the penalties would have been even more severe. It was controversial and opposed by some big guns, so to speak, but we got it through the Assembly repeatedly.

In all those years, the Senate never even brought the bill to the floor for debate or a vote. To this day, the bill I wrote continues to be active with a new sponsor and is overwhelmingly approved by the Assembly at least annually. But the New York State Senate continues to vote it down. This isn't an anti-gun bill. Safe storage of a firearm is about prevention, not eliminating the right to own a firearm. Guns don't kill people, people do. People have to prevent access of a loaded firearm to any child at any time. Due to the negligence we continue to read about today with horrific consequences, it makes no sense that there are those who have access to guns that can kill or injure others.

Something else, also a lifesaver, but in a very different way, that I was able to accomplish was securing a grant for the Long Beach Breast

Cancer Coalition. I was featured in the newspaper, along with the Coalition's founders, Long Beach Supervisor Bruce Nyman, Sue Rosenbaum, and Marylou Monahan.

During 1993, we saw horrible incidents of bias around the Island, including anti-Semitic graffiti in Oceanside. In November of that year, I was the keynote speaker at an interfaith service, sponsored by the Kiwanis Club and hosted by The People's Church of Long Beach. Clergy of all faiths from all over the barrier island were in attendance, as were public officials. "The climate in the room was just beautiful," I was quoted as saying. "You could feel the love and compassion. There was a sense of solidarity."

I also attended a meeting on the subject hosted by the Five Towns Jewish Council. I advocated for the only solution I thought made sense. "What we have to do," I said, "is to make the parents of the vandals financially responsible for what they do." This, of course, in addition to any punishment meted out by the legal authorities.

Prior to the 1993 holidays, Congressman Peter King and I placed an ad in the newspaper asking that people "Join us in a community wide show of solidarity against bias," and to place a lighted candle in their windows on January 3, 1994. I strongly believe we must have zero tolerance for bigotry of any kind, and this was a powerful symbol in support of that.

Ellen and I traveled twice to the small, poor, rural village of Naguabo in Puerto Rico, which was the hometown of an Assembly member. The people of this village, who had so little, welcomed us warmly and treated us to a beautiful musical performance. I made a modest personal donation of a radio to the town when we learned that the kids loved music, but didn't have a way to listen to it. I was so moved by their response, that I asked the superintendent of schools at the time to join our schools to theirs, as sister schools, thus broadening the horizons of all. "All children are God's children," I said. "And sharing our culture will enrich us all." For a time Long Beach schools participated.

I nominated our wonderful program, Project Challenge, to be a recipient of the 1993 Eleanor Roosevelt Community Service Award, sponsored by First Lady Matilda Cuomo. Project Challenge provides drug prevention aid to neighborhood youth. They were, in fact, one of the winners. The award was presented by the First Lady to founder John White on December 14 at the Omni Albany Hotel.

One of the things I enjoyed about this time in the Assembly was the opportunity to be close to Mario Cuomo and his family. Matilda was a lady to be admired for her interest in the arts and her willingness to help people.

1994—Fishing and Water Safety

In March 1994, I co-sponsored a bill that was controversial within the disparate interests of the fishing community. Fishing trawlers were banned from operating near inlets, Peconic Bay and portions of Gardiners Bay and Long Island Sound. The intent was to provide sport fishermen with bigger catches of fluke and winter flounder. "The intent of the bill is to increase the number of fish in the bays," said Nicholas T. Castoro, president of the New York State Sportfishing Federation, which backed the law and claimed that commercial fishermen "choked off" the inlets.

The bill was opposed by Jim Mangano of the East Hampton Baymen's Association, who said, "It's hard to say how much we can take." The bill banned commercial fishing within two miles of Jones and Fire Island Inlets and one-and-a-half miles from Shinnecock, Moriches, Rockaway, and East Rockaway inlets.

To help Jones Beach lifeguards ensure beach safety, I worked with Republican State Senators Owen Johnson and Ralph Marino to secure $137,000 to provide a much-needed upgrade to their equipment, including walkie-talkies and two pickup trucks equipped to handle surf rescue equipment and a dozen surf rescue dories, which are small boats. Prior to that time, lifeguards, including myself, were communicating via hand signals and whistles and transporting victims in flatbed garbage trucks.

It was with deep concern that I prepared for another summer of lifeguarding on our beaches. It was and is imperative that we are guaranteed to have lifeguards on all open water beaches, and as the chair of the Assembly Subcommittee for the Protection of Long Island Barrier Beaches, I was determined to do something about it. So I sponsored a bill guaranteeing exactly that. "Who the heck is supposed to be watching the people if the Health Department is saying you don't need lifeguards?" I was quoted in the paper as saying.

I was at the Albany Omni Hotel for Lifeguard Lobbying Day and told stories of some of the lives I have saved, including one day when

I helped save nine people. Tourism is a source of money, and Long Island beaches, particularly Jones Beach, are a big part of that. I just don't think state officials who live far away from the beach understand the importance of our beaches, and that lifeguarding is a serious, critical job, rather than a part-time past time. "We send all our money to the state," I said, and need to get back our fair share.

On Police Recognition Day, May 22, 1994, at one in the afternoon, along with representatives of every police agency in the area, I dedicated the tall, free-standing clock in front of the Long Beach train station on West Park Ave., along with a plaque dedicated to those who served and those who continue to serve. Recently I made another donation as the clock had stopped, and it was important to me that it be repaired. Unfortunately, no one else cared so I withdrew my donation.

I secured $900 for a surf chair, made of white plastic tubing with giant yellow balloon wheels that can maneuver over sand, enabling people with disabilities to enjoy the beach. One of those people was CURB founder Jim Conlon. "I could have cried," Jim said, as he described how his son wheeled him to the shore in the chair. "I bent down and was touching the water. I took my shoes and socks off, and I was like a four-year-old. But I was fifty-two." Ricky has also been able to use these chairs.

I got eight more of these beach chairs for Camp Anchor, where carrying children with disabilities to the water's edge was challenging and dangerous. Lola Reynolds, a Point Lookout mother of four who suffered from multiple sclerosis, used the surf chair to escort her children on the beach every day. "You can't miss me," she said. "Look for the umbrella and the wheels."

I worked with my friend Jim Conlon to make Long Beach as accessible as possible to everyone. "Harvey's done a lot of great things . . . more than any other state or federal official. He's been a part of our project. He's been there when we need him and he not only talks, he acts. If he can't help, he calls someone who can," Jim told one of the newspapers in September 1994.

I also obtained funding for Stephanie Joyce Kahn's Foundation for the blind, and secured a grant to help local merchants make minor renovations for accommodating customers in wheelchairs. I also secured funding for the city to build a wheelchair ramp at the Magnolia Boulevard Beach, so that people in wheelchairs would be able to listen to concerts and use the beach. From curb cuts to ramps, I'm very proud to have made our wonderful city more accessible to all.

I sponsored the South Shore Estuary Reserve act to help protect our beaches. "If we don't have barrier beaches, then Sunrise Highway will become the barrier beach," I said at the time.

The public is understandably cynical about their public officials, many of whom have proven themselves to be talkers, rather than doers. I pride myself on having been different. In 1994, I followed up on a tour of Fire Island with vigorous action to protect that valuable island. I had promised to do so and I kept my promise. I demanded that the state government address the question of erosion control in the area. I lobbied fellow legislators for support and garnered state funding. Yet the pace of progress in the public arena can be slow.

I expressed my frustration about this in the press. "I'm tired of them saying they're going to send out the bird man to check on the birds . . . the sand man to check on the sand," I said. We were then waiting for the Governor to facilitate work to be done by the Army Corps of Engineers. "Just give us a dredge," I pleaded. "We'll do it. We don't need the Army Corps of Engineers."

The Fire Island News put it this way in September 1994: "How did Caesar put it? *Veni, vidi, vici?* I came, I saw, I conquered." One-up on the old Roman is the bipartisan group of state legislators who visited Fire Island after last year's storm, returning for an Island-wide public hearing in Ocean Beach this Friday. They came, they saw, they listened and they acted!" The result was that we made people in Albany aware of our needs.

In October and November 1994, in both Long Beach and the Five Towns, we brought the Department of Motor Vehicles to the people for an early-bird driver's license renewal program to make it more accessible. It was a success. "This can't be the Department of Motor Vehicles," one woman said. "The clerk is smiling."

I was honored to be the Long Beach Chamber of Commerce Man of the Year in 1994. And I won a third term in the Assembly, the end of a very busy year.

1995—A Good Year

When I was in the room with Mario Cuomo, who served as Governor of

New York for three terms, from 1983 to 1994, I knew I was in the room with greatness. We got along very well. I frequently challenged him, and he enjoyed being challenged, and I always did so respectfully— quite a contrast with the way things are often handled nowadays. He called me at home on occasion, complimenting me on bills I sponsored and which he had just signed.

When Republican George Pataki ran for Governor of New York against the three-term incumbent, he was an unknown from upstate. We were friends because we used to work out in the workout room. Pataki was a quiet gentleman.

However, after an article in the paper said that even Democrats in Long Beach didn't show strength for Mario Cuomo, we met on Long Island. I told Cuomo, "You have one hundred members in the Assembly; all you have to do is ask for help." Cuomo answered, "I'm asking now." As the campaign progressed, Long Beach showed a positive interest in him being re-elected. I thought he was a great Governor. We did everything we could. I was disappointed he didn't win.

Pataki defeated Cuomo by a margin of more than three points as part of the Republican revolution of 1994. George Pataki served as the fifty-third Governor of New York, and was sworn in January 1995. The day after his victory, Pataki had a breakfast and invited the Long Island Democrats. I'm the only one who showed up. And George said, "Sit next to me." I had an open-door relationship with Pataki. I got a lot of stuff done with him.

While Mario Cuomo was still Governor, we got $30 million in funding to prepare for the international sports competition, the Goodwill Games. That enabled us to build the Nassau County Aquatics Center pool in East Meadow for the games, which took place in 1998. It is considered to be the largest Olympic-sized single-tank pool in North America. I was the one who debated the bill on the floor. Ironically, the only person who debated me at all about the expense was an Assemblyman from East Rockaway who said it was going to cost too much. Our hope was to one day hold the Olympics here. Fortunately the funding came through.

One area in which Long Beach lagged behind other municipalities in Nassau County was that our residents were not able to vote on school budgets, so I sponsored a bill to change that. "Sixty percent of our property taxes go to fund our school system," I said at the time. "Ten years ago," I said, "Governor [Mario] Cuomo said the State Legislature promised the people of the small city school districts the right to vote on their school budgets." I held him to that promise.

I sponsored a bill, which Governor Pataki, signed, that increased law enforcement presence on our Long Island Railroad trains after a man named Colin Ferguson boarded a train on December 7, 1993 and killed six people. The law also granted free train fare to police officers. The other day I got on the train and showed the conductor my police shield. He told me that police officers still can ride free; they are now issued certificates. A lot of Long Island cops go to work in the city, so I think this is a good benefit.

The year 1995 was also the year that I was able to secure funding to help many of our residents. The list reads: The Five Towns Senior Center; the City of Long Beach Recreation Department; Atlantic Beach Rescue Unit; Long Beach Reach; Parkinson Support Group of Long Island; Lido Beach Synagogue; Link Counseling Center; Beach Young Men's & Young Women's Hebrew Association; Greater Five Towns YM & YWHA; Long Beach Public Library; Lekotek Center (Theresa Foundation); St. Mary of the Isle Church; Long Beach Memorial Hospital; Five Towns Jewish Council; City of Long Beach; Peninsula Counseling Center; City of Long Beach Police Department; Five Towns Child Care Center, Inc.; Long Beach Island Intercultural Community Coalition; United Cerebral Palsy Association of Nassau County; Project Challenge of Long Island; M.L.K. Center; City of Long Beach Fire Department; Oceanside Anti-Bias Committee; City of Long Beach Junior Life Guards; Oceanside Counseling Center; Stephanie Joyce Kahn Foundation; JASA; Circulo De La Hispanidad; Long Island Chapter–Arthritis Foundation; North Shore University Hospital; Long Beach Historical & Preservation Society; Point Lookout Civic Association; Citizens United to Remove Barriers; Anchor; Lido Beach Town Park; and the Long Beach Booster Club.

As I said, a good year.

Another key to a healthy society is healthy infrastructure. I secured $2.4 million for the reconstruction in Long Beach of East Broadway, from Lincoln to Maple Boulevard, from the Suburban Highway Improvement Program (S.H.I.P.S.), including new storm drains, curbs and sidewalks, a new roadbed, and beautiful landscaping. Functional, attractive infrastructure enhances the quality of all our lives.

A project that had been talked about for thirty years was the Fifth Avenue Corridor road raising and route straightening project in East

Rockaway. Residents were frustrated by the lack of progress, as many were constantly being flooded during high tides and storms. At full-moon high tides, the water would come up to people's doors. This was all related to the Bay Park Sewage Treatment Plant. I had received hundreds of letters requesting some support and called a town meeting to see if we could get the people some relief. And we did. A spokesperson for the Town of Hempstead said that the presiding supervisor directed the Nassau County Department of Public Works to meet with the residents, as "he does not want this to get lost in the shuffle of the county legislature." I discovered that an engineer had been tasked with working on the project for eighteen years and could ostensibly retire with a pension without ever having put a shovel in the ground. Can you believe that? The project was completed. This was a great victory.

As I've said earlier in this book, the thank yous I get from people are the real rewards of the job, but occasionally there is a bit of recognition, and that's nice too. Two environmental groups, Environmental Advocates and the Environmental Planning Lobby, jointly published a voter guide, and ranked legislators based on their record on the environment. I received a ninety-six, the highest score in 1995.

In December, with legislators from about six other states, I went (along with Ellen of course) to Europe to study the educational systems of Germany, Austria, and Switzerland. What I found was very much in line with what I had been suggesting for some time; emphasizing technology and skill development so that those who might not have academic achievements can be supported by the system in their efforts to become contributing members of society.

"We have been teaching kids the same way for over a hundred years," I said. "It is time to re-evaluate education as we know it. We need to emphasize academics that will coincide with skill development so we can compete in the global economy." My philosophy of education has always been to develop the whole child, including music and art, along with academic skills, which goes the European model one better.

The trip was a life-changing experience in another way as we also visited Dachau, one of the concentration camps in Germany. The other legislators and I had a graduate student as our guide. Going through the camp and hearing how they disciplined, tortured, and gassed Jews, and seeing the evidence of man's inhumanity to man was horrible. I asked the guide if the people in the communities had known what was happening back then and he said yes. It's still hard to believe, and it's made worse that this bigotry and hatred still exists today.

1996—Education

Our trip to Europe inspired me to take a closer look and take action to make our New York State educational system more directly applicable in the lives of students. In February 1996, I introduced a legislative package consisting of five separate bills to engage parents, communities, and especially businesses in the education process. I believe it is vitally important that education be applicable to one's work, and these bills were specifically geared to what was referred to as "school-to-work" or "career education."

People tended to think of education as existing in two tiers, one for those who were college-bound and the other for those who were not. The latter group is sometimes perceived as being second-class students, but I do not agree with this. Both processes lead to one destination, a career. So I created a School-to-Work system, which was supported on the federal level by then President Bill Clinton, and which gave students access to both school-based and work-based activities; provided fiscal incentives for business participation in school-to-work; allowed districts to extend students beyond grade twelve to ensure they complete both aspects of their education; and required school districts to include career education in their biennial planning.

The School-to-Work Program utilized a $50,000 grant to develop a series of K–12 school-to-career initiatives, both school- and work-based. I've always said that our youth are our future. "We must enable all our young people to become skilled, literate, contributing members of the workforce," I said, speaking as chairman of the Legislative Commission on Skills Development and Vocational Education.

Tuition for a thirteenth year would be waived and local workplace development boards would be created to design programs in vocational education, adult literacy, and workplace apprenticeships. I changed the wording of the law from vocational education to career education, which leveled the playing field in terms of perception. Career education is every bit as important and has every bit as much value as academic education, because it leads to the same result, a career. New York State

Assembly Education Committee Chairman Steve Sanders explained, "One of the most appealing aspects of these bills is that they do not add any new mandates to local school districts. Rather, districts are provided with incentives to participate." In other words, no new taxes.

Protecting young people meant not only focusing on students but helping newborns and their mothers. Pressure on hospitals to fill beds and from insurance companies to hold down the costs of care has led to a disturbing trend of allocating less and less in-hospital time to new mothers and their babies. So I co-sponsored a bill that required hospitals, Health Maintenance Organizations, better known as HMOs, and insurance companies to provide at least forty-eight hours of inpatient care to newborns and their mothers for "normal births," and one-hundred-twenty hours after caesarean sections.

The previous year, in 1995, two users of personal water craft, or PWCs, commonly referred to as Jet Skis or Wave Runners, disappeared off Southampton and were found dead sometime later. I wanted to make sure that our waterways and all who use them are as safe as possible. So I introduced a bill requiring all PWC riders to carry horns audible for a half-mile in calm weather and either three flares or an orange distress flag. PWCs were not subject to the same laws as other watercraft because they were only allowed to be used during daylight hours and the expectation was they would be used only near the shore.

In January, a six-year-old child was struck by a car while trying to cross a street to get on a stopped school bus. Because it was legal to drive across the area in front of a school bus from a side street, the driver in this incident was not even given a ticket. So I introduced a bill proposing that any vehicle approaching to within one hundred feet of a stopped school bus from any direction be prohibited from moving.

To help homeowners cope with rising insurance rates related to storms, I sponsored a bill that provided for a reduction in premiums for properties fitted with hurricane-resistant, shatter-resistant windows and doors. The intent was to keep the high winds of a hurricane from entering homes as a result of broken windows or door panels from the impact of an airborne object.

We also ensured that homeowners would be able to acquire or maintain their insurance coverage for at least one year from the date of a policy cancellation or non-renewal. The original Senate bill did not cover people in high-rise condos and co-ops. It took many meetings to get the Senate to work out an agreement to cover these properties.

"We have taken a significant step in the right direction," I said at the time, "but the issue is far from closed. I am pleased that the introduction of the legislation places a moratorium on cancellations and non-renewals. I hope that this crisis will not be repeated and comprehensive reforms are permanently instituted in the near future."

This bill enabled twenty-five thousand people to be insured who otherwise might have been cut off. "I'm sending a cannon shot across the bow to the insurance industry, which says, if they want to write insurance policies in the state of New York, they have to include everyone at a fair and equal rate," I said at the time.

We held the First Annual Citizens United to Remove Barriers (CURB) fundraising bike tour around Long Beach in 1996, with the late Jim Conlon and Jim Monahan, and, in later years, with Bill Papetti, Matt Demerest, and Casey Kantor. The sixty riders we had that first year has grown exponentially since, and helped countless people have greater access to activities by supplying portable ramps, purchasing motorized wheelchairs, having rails installed in homes, and much more.

I concluded in August of that year that the Long Beach incinerator's emissions posed "a significant threat to the public health and environment," and called in Senator Al D'Amato, who lived in Island Park, within "smelling distance," as the newspapers put it, of the facility, to help see to its closing. The levels of dioxin, a contributor to reproductive disorders and cancer, in the plant's emissions were twenty-one times higher than limits set by the U.S. Environmental Protection Agency. Mercury limits were also unacceptably high. So the plant had to go. But first, I went to visit this facility where I used to shovel coal as a teenager, and I saw products that had Pennsylvania labels on them. They wouldn't burn them there, so why did they think it was okay to burn them in Long Beach? The manager of the incinerator at the time came up to my office to offer me a $1,000 "donation." I tore up his check and threw him out of my office. Bruce Nyman, D'Amato, and I got the plant shut down at the end of March 1997.

I secured the grant that led to the establishment of the Wall of Fame at Long Beach High School on October 18, 1996. The solid oak monument stretched alongside the entire school lobby and honored the many individuals that contributed to our school's success. "The pride that we express in our community is our greatest asset and resource," I said. "We have so much to be proud of."

By the end of this year, I had been elected to a fourth term in the Assembly.

1997—Flags in Every Classroom

The year began with an honor. The Long Beach chapter of the U.S. Lifesaving Association presented me with a lifetime achievement award in February for my work in lifeguarding and beach safety. Among my achievements mentioned was the Jet Ski safety legislation, then being used as a model throughout the nation for other laws.

I sponsored the resolution that established the first annual Police Memorial Day, on May 13, 1997, a day of mourning for those police officers who so bravely gave their lives in the line of duty.

In January, I happened to be visiting a school in New York City, and I looked around and asked an official if they had a flag in the school, so the students would be able to salute the flag. The official pointed to a tiny sticker of a flag on a window. It occurred to me that there was a possibility that not every classroom in every school had a flag, so I had a study done to find out. The results were that many schools did not have a flag to salute in the morning. So I got in touch with Danny Lehner, president of the Nassau Council of Chambers of Commerce, who passionately believed in the issue. Together, this fine gentleman and I gave four thousand American flags to every legislator from both sides of the aisle to distribute to schools they represented. It was Danny who raised the money for the flags. I sponsored a bill to have the Stars and Stripes displayed in classrooms throughout New York State, a measure that passed both houses with flying colors. Literally.

We then honored Danny Lehner in the Assembly. Tragically, the very next day, June 3, Danny had a heart attack while dancing at a rock concert, and died. Danny was what we called a mensch, a real giver. Senator D'Amato, also a friend of Danny's said, "He was a big-hearted man who made charity his first and foremost responsibility. If there was a community need he sought to address it. If there was a person in pain, he sought to provide comfort. His untimely passing leaves an enormous gap in the fabric of Long Island." Well said.

In March, legislation that I introduced to provide homeowners with a reduction in homeowner's insurance for homes fitted with hurricane-resistant glass windows and doors, passed both the State Assembly and State Senate. I also introduced a bill, sponsored by Senator Dean Skelos to provide a reduction in risk insurance for owners of commercial property fitted with shatter-resistant glass windows or doors. The legislation for homeowners was signed into law by Governor Pataki in June.

In May, State legislators finally agreed to revive a crucial, last-resort insurance program and keep it in place until April 30, 1998. The extension fell short of my goal to get the state to put a permanent program in place—something I had continued to fight for since the storm of 1992—but it made it more difficult for insurance companies to withdraw from the homeowner's market.

On a hot August night that year, I got no sleep as I fought to ensure that a very special item remained in the $68 billion New York State budget. The appropriation provided $500,000 for the first home for "medically frail" children. These are children who would not survive without round-the-clock medical attention, often including devices that enabled them to breathe, and in a very real sense allowed them to live. The home gave parents the ability to, at the very least, be near their children, many of whom would die within a few months or a year of being hospitalized. The project was overseen by the Independent Group Home Living Program (IGHLP), the nonprofit agency whose CEO was and is my friend, Walter Stockton.

The home was the first of what are now three at this writing, all named after a young girl whose short life inspired her parents, the Policastros, to spend their lives helping families like theirs, in the name of their daughter, Angela. The founding of Angela's House is one of my proudest achievements, in part because it serves people who, like our Ricky, need help the most. At the time, Ricky was still living at the Long Island Developmental Center in Melville, where Ellen and I could visit with him regularly.

Bob Policastro devoted six years of his life to see such a home established in New York, after having gone through the horror, along with his wife, of watching their one-year-old daughter waste away in an out-of-state facility before passing away from pneumonia.

Angela was born severely brain damaged on August 30, 1989. She spent the first six months of her life in the pediatric intensive care unit of North Shore University Hospital. When she was to be discharged, her parents Bob and Angie couldn't find a facility closer than New Britain, Connecticut, one hundred fifty miles from home. The Policastros visited her there once a week for seven months. But on October 8, 1990, a day before their scheduled visit, they got the call that their daughter had developed a severe case of pneumonia. Before her parents could reach her, she had passed away.

"I vowed that this would not happen to other families," Bob said. "It was hard enough going through this without the added grief of having to travel two-and-a-half hours to see Angela." His family's tragedy has become a kind of saving grace for others. He had lobbied politicians and organized parents of disabled kids for meetings starting in 1992. We met at a breakfast in October 1996, and of course because of what Ricky had been through, the Policastros' story resonated with me. So I called in favors, cornering Governor Pataki and then Senate Majority Leader Joseph Bruno at official events, buttering up the chairmen of the Assembly and the Senate Committees on Mental Health, and inviting myself to meetings with officials of the State Office for People With Developmental Disabilities (OPWDD). Basically I did what I still do best; push people until they say yes.

As I was quoted as saying at the time: "Establishing this type of facility would truly be a Godsend to the families in need of it. While we cannot mend the heartache experienced by parents of medically fragile children, we can help make sure that their children stay close enough to visit and hug every day."

And finally, on that hot August day, I was able to help get the funding to establish the first Angela's House right here on Long Island in East Moriches, which keeps these very ill children closer to home. A second one opened in Smithtown in 2005, and they opened a third one in Stony Brook in 2012.

1998—A Good Year for Long Beach

In January, a consortium of wealthy businessmen asked the City of Long Beach to allow a gambling boat to dock and pick up passengers at a marina here in 1998. Bad idea. Bad bet. Nassau Legislator Bruce Nyman called the idea "insane." I asked City Manager Ed Eaton to ban gambling boats here in much the same way that Freeport had banned them. Gambling-related traffic and parking would have been terrible. "We simply cannot afford to 'roll the dice' with the future with these boats," I said at the time. Long Beach gambling, on boats or on land, was not in the cards. In a previous section, I wrote that in the late 1970s there was talk of bringing in casino gambling to Long Beach, which I initially supported as a means to increase city revenue. But the City Council and I changed our minds back then and nothing has made me think any differently since then.

Environmental issues continued to be a priority for me. The number of sites in New York State requiring environmental remediation grew at an average rate of thirty-five per year. A report by the state's Superfund board cited a lack of money and "legal authority" as two key issues that were part of the "several hundred sites that would lack funds to be remediated," I was quoted as saying in *Newsday* in February 1998. Long Beach had commissioned a cleanup assessment for the half-century-old municipal incinerator, which had been closed a year earlier. Sarah Nichols of the Coalition to Close the Long Beach incinerator had been instrumental in the plant's closing. Sarah expressed concern and cited studies indicating "ash constituents in the soil and upper level ground water."

As part of an agreement to restore and protect nearly one hundred water projects across New York State, I secured over $500,000 for the West Long Beach Sewer District, money that came from the Clean Water/Clean Air Bond Act, a statewide effort for protecting clean waters all over New York. The funding would improve the Sewer District's pollution control system, which would achieve improved reliability and compliance with flow permits and improved maintenance. The project was achieved with the help of Republican Senator Dean Skelos. The use of Reynolds Channel for swimming, boating, and fishing was—and still is—a vital part of our residents' lives. I am proud to have had a hand in protecting these waters.

This was a good year for Long Beach. I helped to allocate $860,000 for our city in state aid, an increase of more than $250,000 over 1997.

Accidents related to Jet Skis continued to be a concern, so I sponsored legislation requiring their operators to pass a day-long, certified safety course designed specifically for that purpose. Educated operators would be "to the industry's benefit," I said at the time. My bill was signed into law by Governor Pataki on July 2, 1998. In 1997 there had been six fatalities involving personal watercraft (PWCs). New York

State had thirty-two thousand registered PWCs with about one-hundred operators in the state. Imagine how many lives we saved with this bill? But it's worth noting that before any of my upstate colleagues would even consider the legislation I proposed, I had to first explain what a Jet Ski was!

That summer I received multiple phone calls that the Town of Hempstead's Camp Anchor had been denying Long Beach residents placement in their program. It had long been an unwritten agreement that our special children would be accepted into the program in exchange for the use of Long Beach schools during Camp Anchor rain dates. A Town of Hempstead spokesperson claimed that the City of Long Beach had not offered its facilities to the Camp Anchor program. Ultimately, I got a $100,000 grant so that the Long Beach School District would be able to set up a program for our special kids to have recreation resources.

The American flag is a symbol of what our country stands for and when I think of the lives lost in protecting our flag and the rights that we have in this country, I think dedicating it to law enforcement, fire departments, veterans, and lifeguards, is an important recognition. That's why one of the numerous flagpoles I have donated is on Route 878 in Inwood, "in Honor of the Civic Association and those who serve to protect their community as police officers and volunteer fire fighters." I donated this flagpole memorial in 1998. I also have one in Woodmere for veterans. In Long Beach on Virginia Avenue there's one for the lifeguards. And I donated one at Ricky's house in Plainview.

I helped to commemorate the 50th Anniversary of AHRC by having a photo representing their history installed at Long Beach City Hall.

In July 1998, portions of Rockaway Beach were closed when lifeguards found syringes and crack vials there. The situation was reminiscent of a decade earlier, when medical waste forced temporary beach closings along the South Shore. While this isolated incident was certainly cause for concern and vigilance, I have always been confident in the beauty of our beaches and our waters. "The water is clean and beautiful," I said in the newspaper. "If you go fifty feet off shore and look into the water, it's just so crystal clear."

In fact, that year there were several forms of marine life that beachgoers could enjoy that hadn't been seen in years. "It's amazing to see the beautiful starfish that end up on the shore," I said at the time. "I haven't seen those in a long while."

So that more people could enjoy an ocean view, I was able to secure fifteen more surf chairs, for a total of sixteen, to make the beaches in District 20 accessible for all.

On September 20, I joined with local students in our Long Beach School District and Legislator Bruce Nyman, and ninety other coastal communities, for the Annual International Coastal Cleanup. We bagged and categorized garbage to help our community understand the impact of garbage on our environment. The challenges we face motivate me and many others to respond in creative, effective ways to make society and all our lives better.

On October 1, I honored the West End Neighbors Civic Association with a flagpole I purchased. It was dedicated that day at the Municipal Lot at the corner of Virginia Avenue and West Beech Street, the former site of the Lucky Twins building, which had been demolished that summer. "The West End Neighbors is thirty-one years old," said organization president, John White, "and we have never been recognized by the City before."

On October 18, at the Garden of Hope on Park Avenue and Roosevelt Boulevard, we held a memorial ceremony in honor of Sue Rosenbaum and all those who have suffered from breast cancer or other cancer-related illnesses. It was the fifth anniversary of the death of Sue Rosenbaum, who had been the first president of the Long Beach Breast Cancer organization. Ellen and I were proud to have donated this beautiful garden as a reminder of all of the people who have been taken from us by this terrible disease.

I also sent every Long Beach resident my pet project; an emergency evacuation plan, "Long Beach Barrier Island Guide to Emergency Preparedness and Evacuation." I had organized and paid for it. As I told residents at the time, it had become my personal baby since the December hurricane of 1992 "because the reality is if we ever do get hit here, we could lose tens of thousands of lives." I had also finally, after three years of trying, gotten blue coastal evacuation route signs all over the island. There are only three ways to leave Long Beach; the Atlantic Beach Bridge, the Long Beach Bridge, and the Loop Parkway-Meadowbrook Parkway. Some people said that those of us who were worried about this sounded like Chicken Little. But my job is to protect my constituents even when they don't foresee what I can. So I also secured funding for special equipment in case of flooding and training for firefighters on how to use it. Though it would be several more years before Sandy hit us, I know that the work I did in 1998 with the support of City Council members helped to prepare us for that future storm.

And in November in a landslide, I won a fifth term in the Assembly. That was after I told my opponent Phil Steinberg simply: "I do not campaign. I do my job, and if you do your job the people elect you. I've always been visible and available." That was what the newspapers called "the battle of the 'bergs.'" In politics, you have to take the humor where you can get it.

1999—More Drug-Free Education

At the start of 1999, I was appointed chairman of the Assembly Committee of Alcoholism and Substance Abuse. My background in both drug prevention education and law enforcement prepared me well for this important post. Upon my appointment, I vowed to focus on prevention and treatment rather than incarceration and punishment. I also vowed to be open to input from others across the state who were working to rid our children and families from the destructive and heinous grip of substance abuse. Since my tenure at Bowling Green, I had continued to be involved in anti-drug programs, participating in numerous conferences, including a New York State Regional Conference on a Drug-Free America and a White House Conference on a Drug-Free America.

Soon after, I launched an investigation into the sale of alcohol over the Internet to minors in New York State. "It is appalling," I said upon learning of the issue, "that any youngster with access to a computer can illegally obtain beer, wine, and hard liquor. The phenomenal growth of commerce on the Internet is largely a very positive enterprise," I noted. As a state we had done much to address alcohol and drug abuse, but we must move swiftly to see that our efforts are not undermined by cyber sales, I said, urging my colleagues to join me in the effort.

Sometimes you have to protect the protectors, in this case, guide dogs. Following reports in the *Albany Times Union* of a vicious attack on a guide dog, I introduced a bill making it illegal to mishandle a dog in such a way that it attacks a guide dog. And I made sure the measure, like the canines whose attacks we were addressing, had real teeth, as in financial penalties for the owners. Guide dogs are taught, at a cost of

$25,000, to not only be of invaluable assistance to their owners, but to be non-aggressive, putting them at a severe disadvantage if attacked by a vicious dog. The trauma of such an attack on both dog and owner is incalculable. The least we could do for these valuable companions is to protect them with the force of law. We passed the bill with the help of Senator Majority Leader Joseph Bruno of Albany.

I had February named Childhood Cancer Awareness Month in honor of Lucas and Zachary Powell, five-year-old twins from Brentwood, who had died in 1997 from a rare form of leukemia. The chief cause of death by disease in children under age fifteen was cancer, so calling attention to the thousands of children with cancer was of the utmost importance.

In their memory, I helped families, doctors, and the hospital fund set up a suite of rooms in which parents could stay with their sick children at Stony Brook University Medical Center. Parents told me heartbreaking stories of their sick children, with depleted immune systems, staying in rooms with other sick children, and of the parents sleeping in doorways to be as close as they could be to their kids.

I submitted a letter to the Speaker and the Governor requesting that $220,000 be included in the state budget to fully address this issue. And that's exactly what happened. When we dedicated the suite—the newly named Powell room—which included a kids' game room, we had children holding their IV poles, nurses, doctors, and family there as well. When we cut the ribbon in 2000, there wasn't a dry eye in the room. Such was the relief that these families could now be together, and the children would not have to suffer alone. It was also an example of how we can find resources not for political reasons because this wasn't going to impact me politically. It was about public service, which is what the Legislature is all about.

Also in February, I obtained a $90,000 grant to build Nassau County's first Municipal Skateboard Park right here in Long Beach, along the Reynolds Channel waterfront on ten thousand square feet of what had been a parking lot between Magnolia and National Boulevards. In part this was done to enhance the waterfront park's already existing sports facilities, including the basketball and tennis courts—all in line with my belief that Long Beach is about recreation. But it was also a safety measure in response to the need for a supervised site for kids to skateboard following a 1998 incident in which two boys were hit by a LIRR train in

Island Park as they crossed the tracks with their skateboards. The boys spent several months in the hospital before being released. My daughter Vicki knew one of them. The park opened in October 1999 and had the participation of Long Beach high recent graduate Mike Flammer, who is an artist and skateboarder; he helped design the park.

We received nearly $500,000 in "accelerated" state funds in early 1999, meaning the money came to us earlier than it might have otherwise. As I said at the time, the city was "happy to have it." I also garnered $308,402 through the Consolidated Highway Improvement Program (CHIPS) for the 1999-2000 budget, to "help the City of Long Beach in keeping the roads safe for the residents of our area," I explained.

The modified handicapped ramp at the boardwalk on New York Avenue and a second ramp over the dunes on Tennessee opened "up a new world for many," I told the press at that time. Our physically challenged residents were the primary reason for considering these ramps. But they were and remain amenities for babies in strollers and the elderly, who would enjoy these gateways to access to the shore with relative ease. I was able to help my friends Councilwoman Pearl Weill, Councilman Scott Nigro and Jim Conlon of CURB with $40,000 in funding for the projects.

Though I am very much a Long Beach guy, I am proud to have actively represented all of my constituents. I obtained a $25,000 grant for the Five Towns Community Chest in 1999, to help The Five Towns Senior Center adopt the structural changes needed to comply with the Americans With Disabilities Act. Thirty seven percent of Five Towns residents at that time were between the ages of sixty and eighty-five. My grant helped many of them access services that demonstrably improved their quality of life.

Sometimes my work revolved around just one person. Can you imagine not being able to hear music? Or your loved one express his or her love? Or your child's laughter? I helped a little girl, Carly Howard, receive a cochlear implant, which allowed her to hear for the first time, at a time when the Nassau County BOCES program for hearing impaired youngsters was nearly closed. I could not believe that I found myself arguing with people who thought it best that children who were born deaf stay that way. These children face enough of an uphill battle, without having the State Education Department make life even more difficult for them.

Carley's parents are Hugh, a former fire chief, and Dawn, an outstanding Oceanside teacher, and together they gave me a plaque with Carly's picture on which these words were written: "Thank you for letting me hear the world." That about says it all. With her parents' love and support, Carly graduated high school, attended college, and is both an outstanding student and athlete, not to mention a terrific young lady. Recently, I saw her parents and they told me to look for an invitation to her wedding.

In May, the Long Beach Recreation Center got a much-needed facelift thanks to an infusion of funds I had arranged from the State's Community Enhancement Facilities Assistance Program. This lively hub had been around since my Uncle Buster had first developed it in the 1950s and it had been a prominent part of my life as well. So it was important to me to help the city move ahead with a revitalization plan—especially because in this case it included greater access for the physically challenged. The $160,000 grant paved the way for many improvements, including the installation of a wheelchair lift so physically challenged residents could access the pool easily from the locker rooms and steam rooms, and the entire facility was to be enhanced to remove any barriers to access.

And in a wonderful conclusion to the heart-breaking Policastro story, as I referenced earlier in this chapter, there was a groundbreaking ceremony on the first Angela's House in August, located in East Moriches. One of the best parts of my many years of service is the fruition of the hard-won fights I have been a part of. For the Policastos, this was the reward for ten long years of persistence.

In an interview in the spring 1999 newsletter of the Independent Group Home Living Program, Inc., I said that I don't think of myself as a politician. In fact, I hate politics. I don't have the patience for how government works. When I see a situation where the government clearly has an opportunity—and an obligation—to fulfill a need, then I think we should provide money to satisfy that need. I don't worry about whether it's going to get me more or fewer votes. I've been elected time and again because the people who vote for me see that I fight for what's right, regardless of whether I'm a Democrat or a Republican. And part of what's right is to provide for those who are less fortunate. As my time in politics passed into a new century, these sentiments became even more pronounced.

Ellen and me at the opening of the Harvey Weisenberg Resource Center (HWRC) in Old Bethpage in 2007.

A most meaningful thank you from Cardinal Timothy Dolan for my work with people with special needs.

Happy Birthday, Ellen. The tradition I started, to leave flowers on every New York State Assembly member's desk on her birthday, June 15, continued the June after she passed away.

Ricky, Ellen, and me, enjoying a concert at Long Beach. It is something we did all summer as Ricky responded to the music.

Adoption day April 19, 2010 with Ellen, Ricky, and me; the happiest day to be with our son.

Lifeguarding, a career I have enjoyed for over sixty years and continue to this day.

I'm always connecting with new groups who advocate for special folks. Members and athletes from the Challenged Athletes Foundation in California enjoyed a Surf for All day in Long Beach in 2018.

Future lifeguards, including the grandchildren of some of my friends, in a safety lifesaving course at Long Beach Municipal Pool in summer 2018.

I still participate each year in the Skudins' Surf for All program, which gives children and adults of all abilities the chance to surf. This is the end of another happy program in the summer of 2018.

Mary Margaret Quinn, who died at age sixteen, was an angel and just one of the many special children who have touched my life and inspired my work. She enjoyed our surf program.

The garden I planted in Ellen's memory at the corner of Grand Boulevard and Broadway in Long Beach. The plaque reads: "In memory of Ellen Weisenberg. Her love and empathy for our community and its people, especially for those with special needs, will remain her legacy. Her beauty and elegance will blossom every spring in this garden and live on in our hearts."

7.

State Assembly, 2000–2014

After ten years of serving the 20th District by traveling from Long Beach to Albany for the 380-mile round trip, Ellen and I had a routine. She would accompany me during the week. We'd drive up on Sunday and stay until Thursday night. We stayed in the same Comfort Inn along the New York State Thruway, where we had free parking and breakfast, and I got to use the gym and swim in the pool. The cost was affordable and it became a home away from home, so to speak.

As for my time in the State Capital, I called it Planet Albany. The State Assembly is stressful. It puts wear and tear on your health and well-being. You don't eat properly because of the schedule. You don't sleep properly because you lay in bed thinking about all you have to do to get something done. But the pain is worth the gain when what you lost sleep over, turns into life-changing laws and grants for people who need it most. My next fourteen years in the Assembly turned out to be exactly that.

2000—Honors and Progress

My year started with the ribbon-cutting on January 27 of the respite rooms at Stony Brook Hospital for families like the Powells. But I knew this was only the start of a much bigger effort for more respite facilities for families of extremely ill children being treated for cancer and cancer-related illnesses, so I wrote letters to Governor Pataki and Assembly Speaker Sheldon Silver requesting that $200,000 be included in the State budget to fully fund the remainder of this project.

As a former police officer, I am especially proud of our ability as law enforcement officers to be able to educate young people about the consequences of at-risk behavior, especially using illegal drugs and the abuse of alcohol. It is important for our young people to understand that police officers work on their behalf, as friends, to safeguard our society and the young people themselves, from such behavior. That was something I believed in and strove for when I was a twenty-three-year-old beat officer—and something I still feel strongly about today.

That's why in the challenging arena of alcohol and drug abuse and at-risk behavior some of our young people engage in, I have contributed by creating and coming to the aid of many programs that have addressed this issue. One such program is the DARE (Drug Resistance and Education) program, which first began in Los Angeles in 1983 with the premise that police officers can teach students about the consequences of drug use. In Long Beach it was first taught by Officer Thomas Rourke and was a staple in all our elementary schools for years. I was able to secure the program a $100,000 grant in 2000, and was photographed with a group of DARE students in May of that year. "This makes us solvent, solid for years to come," said Officer James Larsen, one of the program teachers.

When you are as connected to a community as I am to Long Beach, there will inevitably be tragedies that, though painful, bind us together. One that stands out for me is the death of a young man who was smart, tough, and talented. John Kabelka was bigger than life in that he was a wonderful athlete and a talented singer known as Johnny Angel for the band of the same name. He was a good looking kid, and one of my son Russell's best friends. I'll never forget the shock when we learned that the single engine Piper in which he was traveling disintegrated over a frat house at Washington and Lee University in Lexington, Virginia. He was seen hanging from the plane before falling to his tragic death.

Johnny Angel went home at age forty-two. His family wrote a touching letter to the editor in the local paper. "A special thanks to John's best friend, Russell Weisenberg and his father Harvey for their tribute to our son and brother . . . John had wonderful friends and his family appreciated your remembrances more than words could ever express." The power of community is the only thing that can help make sense of tragedies like this one.

In the scheme of things, you might not think of parking as one of life's great difficulties, but the little bits of impact the lack of parking has on our lives on a regular basis can really add up. So it was gratifying indeed to be able to appear at a press conference with State Senator Dean Skelos, City Manager Bruce Nyman, Director of Planning and Development Glen Spiritis, and Long Island Railroad Acting President Kenneth Bauer to announce that we had secured nearly one million for a new parking facility that would as much as double the available commuter parking in Long Beach. It would also beautify the area with landscaping and other aesthetic improvements. If you are one of the many people who parks in this facility, think for a moment about all of the days, many in rain, cold wind, or snow, you would have to leave early enough to find a space. Isn't it nice not to have to do that?

The Hofstra Alumni Association honored me for my public service later that month when I was presented with the 40th Annual George M. Estabrook Distinguished Service Award. I was in good company, as I truly admire all of the recipients of this prestigious award. In November, the Long Beach Chamber of Commerce honored me as Man of the Year, and the National Jewish Women Peninsula Section honored me with the Hannah G. Solomon Award for my consistent commitment and service to children and youth. It's nice to be thanked for the work we do.

In November 2000, I found an interesting use for my former career in track, as *Newsday* reported under a headline that read "Politician Chases Down Suspect." On the Sunday following Election Day, when I won my sixth consecutive term, I was driving in Long Beach and saw a burglary suspect drop his knapsack and flee from a police officer. Foreseeing that he would run to the bus terminal, I gave chase in that direction. Keep in mind, I was sixty-six years old at the time and the suspect, I later learned, was thirty-three. But I was a state quarter-mile champ and my pride was on the line. So I chased him down, caught him, and turned him over to the officer. He was arraigned soon after by Judge Roy Tepper. You never know when past pursuits and accomplishments will come in handy. In my case, I've been lucky numerous times to be able to pull from my past to help the present—something I'm grateful for.

In 2000, there were six-hundred licensed alcoholism programs and seven-hundred licensed substance abuse programs in New York State, and on any given day there were one hundred twenty thousand clients or patients of those programs. I sponsored a bill that combined the two, streamlining treatment by reducing administrative and overhead costs, duplication of monitoring and paperwork, while increasing the flexibility for providers to deliver high-quality, diversified services. The Office of Alcohol and Substance Abuse Services (OASAS) was now able to issue one chemical dependence license for both alcoholism and substance abuse.

I was able to secure a $25,000 grant for an important program that served local students at Project Challenge here in Long Beach. In a nice letter to the editor, John White, the executive director, expressed his thanks and wrote that "this grant certainly saved Project Challenge's Tutoring After School Kids (TASK) program for the year. Over one-hundred youngsters will continue to be served, possibly saved daily because of this program." This grant was particularly significant because in 2001 the program lost twenty percent of its funding. "This truly demonstrates how important Assemblyman Weisenberg's grant is to us," John wrote. "It also shows how important it is to have a concerned leader in Albany working for our children. Thank you again, Harvey!"

2001—A Significant Year of Change for All

One of the biggest challenges in education is determining how we measure student and teacher success. Pressure to standardize testing and "teach to the test," is nothing new. My summer of 2001 newsletter addressed this issue. ". . .schools have changed their curricula to match the test material, forcing teachers to teach to the tests," I wrote. "Every child is different and learns best in different ways . . . We should measure the ability of our schools by how well they develop the potential of each student." The problem, I said then, and I say it now, is that many of those in the education community forget that the purpose of our schools is teaching, not testing.

Our students also absolutely must be safe in school. "We're dealing with a very violent society," I was quoted as saying in the newspapers in March 2001. I hate to say it, but it's true. Bullying has been a scourge in our schools for a long time. Kids can be cruel, and so I believe it's important for those of us in public service to afford all persons in public schools an environment free of harassment and discrimination based on actual or perceived race, national origin, ethnic group, religion, mental or physical disability, sexual orientation, or gender. I was able to get a $10,000 grant from New York State to help combat school violence through the Extended Day School Violence Prevention Program, which still exists today.

Just as it's so important to safeguard our school children, it's equally vital to protect our infants. So, following a series of chilling stories of abandoned newborns who died, I sponsored the Abandoned Infant Protection Act, which made it possible for parents who abandon newborns to avoid prosecution if they leave their babies at a safe haven, such as a hospital or police station. Hospitals, pharmacies, and all health care providers would be required to give information about the law to patients seeking prenatal or gynecological services, and notices about the law would be conspicuously posted at related facilities. We passed a law that placed our focus where it belongs; on protecting the baby, not prosecuting the mother.

I also improved the safety of day care centers in New York State by requiring facilities to develop and enact visitor control procedures, which was mandated in order for a facility to obtain or renew its license. Under the law, for the first time, visitors had to be checked in and be at the facility for a legitimate purpose.

I was involved in a terrific program sponsored by the National Cleaners Association called Coats for Kids. This thing really took off, and is a great example of how everyone having their hearts in the right place and giving a little bit can have real impact and help a lot of people. The idea was for people to donate coats so that others who might otherwise have to endure the cold winter might be a little warmer. My office reached out to our community to make people aware of the program. Dry cleaners throughout our community voluntarily cleaned the coats we collected, which numbered more than a thousand. Coats were separated by size and gender, and given to legislators and nonprofits for distribution throughout our region, even going so far as New York City. The event was organized by Arthur Epstein, chairperson for the Coats for Kids Foundation and also continues all these years later.

One of our city's hidden gems is Ocean View, the lovely roadway between West Beech Street and the beach that runs west of New York Avenue. Ocean View had been neglected and was in disrepair and City Manager Bruce Nyman, who was all for repairing Ocean View, lamented that "such a project was unlikely as the city's road repair monies were tied up in canal street projects." Well, I was able to secure $575,000 in state funds to repave Ocean View. "The money is there," I assured a group of West End residents. "It won't be used for anything else." And that's exactly what we did.

Also, with the addition of a handicapped ramp at Virginia Avenue the summer before, by spring 2000, we were among the most handicapped accessible communities in the state.

In June, I stepped up my crusade to make people aware—and care—about my eighth attempt to get a law passed for a clear expiration date on sunscreen and sun-block products sold in New York State. This all started many years before when I was given a bag of sunscreen lotions while working as a lifeguard, and I noticed that one had no expiration date. I brought the product to a pharmacy who informed me that this sunscreen was more than ten years old. And so began my crusade to have expiration dates required on sunscreen and sunblock packaging, along with my career of gracing a billboard on Rockaway Turnpike and Brookville Road, wearing only a Speedo bathing suit.

I was sixty-seven years old. On June 1, I put up the billboard in my district urging residents to check the date. It read: Has Your Sunscreen Expired? Save Yourself! Check for an expiration date. Prevent Skin Cancer. I used my own campaign money for the billboard, which cost $10,000 for three months. The sign actually stayed up until October 2006.

Embarrassing, you say? Worthwhile, I think, when you consider that thousands and thousands of people saw the billboard and were made aware of the perils of skin cancer. Did you know that a person dies every hour from melanoma? One of them was my own beloved Ellen, who had been a lifeguard in high school. Blonde with beautiful, hazel eyes; we could not know at that time, of the pain, suffering, and ultimately the loss of her life in 2016, caused by the sun, which we had loved so much.

I passed this bill unanimously in the Assembly for many years, but the Senate would not consider the bill because of the opposition of one manufacturer, Estee Lauder, which had Long Island-based affiliations. There are expiration dates on water, but not suntan lotion and sunblock. Terrible!

The Colette Coyne Melanoma Awareness Campaign (CCMAC) held annual events to foster awareness of this horrific disease. Family members of people with melanoma would attend these events, sometimes with pictures that showed the awful wounds and scarring of those who are afflicted; sometimes the sick family member would be present.

Many of my colleagues in the Assembly shared with me some of the details of the painful deaths of their loved ones from melanoma.

It wasn't until June 2014 that the Senate finally passed my bill, which was sent to then Governor Andrew Cuomo, who vetoed the legislation in December of that year. It is very sad that this bill was vetoed, because its purpose was only to inform and educate people, to protect them from getting a severe burn that might lead to melanoma. Subsequently our Governor personally witnessed in his significant other, an admired, beautiful lady Ellen and I had the pleasure of meeting, the same pain with the same difficult treatments I saw my poor Ellen suffer. I can only hope that this terrible experience might move Governor Cuomo to reconsider and enact this vital, lifesaving legislation. To this day it has still not become a law, but I keep lobbying for it.

I was deeply moved to be honored by four organizations whose work I have long respected, admired, and supported because of the huge impact they have on the lives of others. I received an award from the Clubhouse of Nassau and Suffolk Counties founded by members of the Alliance for the Mentally Ill, in recognition of my efforts to break down the walls of stigma that have long existed for people with mental illness.

In June, I received the 2001 AHRC Humanitarian Award for my advocacy for people with developmental disabilities, and for helping them to live full and happy lives, and to be part of communities.

In September, I received the 2001 Award for Alumni Achievement from Hofstra University, which is given to alumni who have distinguished themselves in their chosen fields. "My education at Hofstra University has been key to my success as an educator and as a public servant," I said, upon receiving the award. Ellen and I were also honored at the 8th Annual Rod Gilbert Golf Classic to benefit the Diabetes Research Institute for our many years of supporting diabetes research. These thank yous mean a great deal to me, not because I want awards, but because they are benchmarks and evidence of the progress we have made.

Not long after the horror of September 11, 2001, I wrote a column in my newsletter that had originally been intended to honor three firefighters who had lost their lives, including Harry Ford, the late husband of my friend, Legislator Denise Ford. Rather than write something from memory, my thoughts and feelings are more accurately communicated by producing excerpts from that letter, as it appeared in my November newsletter of 2001.

Dear Friends and Neighbors:

The past two months have been almost surreal. Sometimes it feels as though the earth has shifted beneath us. Each of us, in our own way, has struggled to come to grips with the magnitude of the horror, of the loss of human life, and of the sheer evil of the events of September 11th. Yet in the face of the unthinkable, the thing that makes us so American—our perseverance and commitment to our way of life—has not diminished. Our hearts have been broken but not our spirits.

As a public official, I find myself driven to do everything I can to heal our community after this terrible intrusion on our way of life. I cannot say enough about the outstanding leadership of Mayor Rudolph Giuliani and Governor George Pataki.

I had planned to dedicate this newsletter to the memories of the three courageous firefighters who made the ultimate sacrifice on June 17, 2001, Father's Day, when a blaze led to a deadly explosion in Queens. Now, although it is still almost incomprehensible, I also dedicate this newsletter to their 347 brethren: rescue workers lost at the World Trade Center tragedy. We will be forever grateful for and inspired by their unconditional commitment to safeguarding others. We lost almost 6,000 [sic] that day, but with the help of New York City's finest and bravest, 25,000 people were saved—an extraordinary feat.

We are a strong, freedom-loving, and diverse people. We have faced difficult times before and together, we will persevere.

Below is the Fireman's Prayer contributed to my newsletter by the Oceanside Fire Department:

When I am called to duty, God
Wherever flames may rage,
Give me strength to save some life,
Whatever be its age.

Help me embrace a little child,
Before it is too late,
Or save an older person from
The horror of that fate.
Enable me to be alert
And hear the weakest shout,
And quickly and efficiently,
Put the fire out.
I want to fill my calling and,
To give the best of me;
To guard my every neighbor and,
Protect his property.
And if according to my fate,
I am to lose my life,
Please bless with Your Protecting hand
My children and my wife.

A beautiful reflection of how we felt after that horrific day.

I attended many of the funerals of those who were lost from our region, quite a few with Mayor Giuliani, and I felt the pain of those who had lost their loved ones, some of whom I knew personally. The last funeral that I attended was a service without a body. After that, I could not bring myself to attend any more services, and I never stopped dreaming about that family and their loss. That's the truth.

2002—Defibrillator Bill

The 2002 Assembly Session was opened by Rabbi Kenneth Hain of Congregation Beth Shalom in Lawrence, a wonderful, loved, and respected community leader.

The prayerful opening helped to prepare me for all the work that had to be done that year. According to the American Heart Association in 2002, as many as one hundred thousand deaths a year could be prevented with the widespread use of defibrillators, which are small, portable devices that can be used to save lives with minimal training, in the event that CPR fails. As I have witnessed so many times, one family's tragedy, in this case, the loss of a beloved young man, fourteen-year-old Louis Acampora, saved the lives of countless individuals.

I read an article about Louis, a lacrosse player at Northport High School on Long Island, who suffered sudden cardiac arrest and died after being hit in the chest with a lacrosse ball. I learned that Louis was surrounded by faculty, students, and spectators who were trained in CPR, which was administered. But a defibrillator was the only thing that could have possibly started his heart again. This tragedy might have been averted had a defibrillator been made available at that time. The chance of resuscitation decreases by ten percent every minute after the onset of sudden cardiac arrest.

As a former coach, I called his devastated family to express my condolences. After some time, and working with Louis' parents, John and Karen Acampora, we began drafting legislation to prevent this from happening to another family. With the help of Senator John R. Kuhl, an upstate Republican, the bill passed both houses in March and was signed by the Governor in May. When the bill was debated on floor of the Assembly, one Assemblyman raised concerns about this "unfunded mandate" being too costly. I asked him to yield for a question and I said, "How much is a child's life worth?" That was the end of the debate.

Today we have defibrillators in all schools, buildings where a thousand or more people gather, libraries, trains, planes, health clubs, and gyms. The loss suffered by John and Karen Acampora certainly saved a multitude of lives by leading to New York's requiring automated, external defibrillators (AEDs) and staff to ensure their operation in many public places. New York's adoption of my bill led the way for the rest of the country to follow suit. As of today, all fifty states have enacted defibrillator use laws or adopted regulations, and there continue to be frequent adjustments.

I went to Washington with Ellen to a national survivors' conference, where we received an ovation for having our legislation passed and defibrillators put in our schools. These newly required defibrillators saved not only children, but also parents, grandparents, teachers, administrators, and other staff. I was so moved by this meaningful success that I called Governor Pataki to thank him for signing my bill. Since that time, the Acompora family, who have set up a foundation, and I, have been made aware of so many people whose lives have been saved by defibrillators.

Nowadays, I find it disturbing that the trend is to offer fewer services for people with disabilities, and, in the case of places for our special citizens to live the trend is even more pronounced. On May 3, 2002, I sponsored the opening of a home for disabled adults for United Cerebral Palsy on Minnesota Avenue right here in Long Beach. We dedicated the home to my terrific colleague, Republican Assemblyman Phil Healey, who I know would have been proud of the home, which continued to operate until October 2012 and Hurricane Sandy.

On Sunday, May 5, 2002, I was proud to dedicate a bench on the boardwalk to my former colleague, a very good, yet tough Assembly-woman, Eileen Dugan. The plaque on the bench read: "In Memory of NYS Assemblywoman Eileen Dugan, whose love of the beach and ocean was second only to her love of the people she served." I truly do think of my colleagues in the State Assembly as a family. We were so much a part of one another's lives. Working together to help people will do that: bring you together with colleagues who serve the same ideals. Honoring Eileen was a way to recognize that. I have frequently dedicated benches to people who have made a difference in the lives of others—and in my own. Take a walk along the Long Beach boardwalk to see them for yourself.

May 18, 2002 was the first bike ride benefitting the CURB organiza-tion's Fantasy Program, which provides ramps, wheelchairs, medical equipment, entertainment, and rent assistance for people with disabili-ties who cannot afford these items.

On August 19 at ten in the morning, we held the ribbon-cutting ceremony on Maryland Avenue and Ocean View to celebrate the $650,000 reconstruction of this unique and beautiful thoroughfare, which included new sewers, storm drains, curbs, sidewalks, repaving, and a widening of the road by nearly three feet. While I am proud of securing the funding for this important project, I am equally proud of ensuring that the money was spent on this and only this endeavor, as there were efforts to utilize the funding elsewhere in our city. "This ribbon cutting is in recognition of the hard work and persistence of everyone involved with making this project a success," said Long Beach City Council Vice President Scott Nigro. If you haven't had the opportunity to enjoy this charming feature of our city, please do visit Ocean View. It's lovely!

I was also able to secure a $200,000 grant for the Lawrence School District 15, $50,000 of which I felt it vitally important to be used to mod-ify what was then a single-lane driveway into and out of the Peninsula

Public Library, which was owned by the district. The parking lot was too small, and the driveway was an accident waiting to happen for a library serving more than fourteen thousand cardholders (at the time) and a school district of thirty-two students. Those who use this vitally important community resource must be able to do so in a safe manner, and a one-way driveway is not the way.

Libraries have been unsung heroes to our communities since Ben Franklin created the first library centuries ago. In that spirit, I introduced legislation creating a Mill Brook library funding district in Hempstead for this Valley Stream community, which is alongside the Green Acres Mall, as well as a Hewlett Harbor library funding district in the Village of Hewlett Harbor. I am also proud to have been a part of the opening of the Island Park Library, a beautiful facility, which opened in September 2002.

I secured $100,000 for roadwork on Grand Boulevard in Long Beach, at St. Ignatius Church, making it safer for congregants and the students of Long Beach Catholic Regional School. I also secured $50,000 for the Yeshiva in Lawrence to improve the condition of McNeil Avenue near that school. The safety of drivers and pedestrians near our religious schools and houses of worship are of vital importance.

As I've mentioned before, the rewards of public service are the thank yous and a thank you in rhyme, well, even better. Here's one I received in late 2002 from the Come Alive Program, which served seniors in the Five Towns:

To say that you are special would be the understatement of the year!
You work miracles with your honesty and lack of fear.

When you see something that is wrong, you work tirelessly in other's
   hearts to put a song.
You share your gifts with our program "Come Alive,"
To insure that our friends grow and thrive.
You care, you share, you dare to give your love and commitment
   to our seniors all the time,
You visit and inspire us with your warmth and honest smile.
So thank you for being who you are,
To all of us you are a model of hope, a shining star!

Blessings from above with our hearts and soul, for you make us feel
   important,
You make us feel whole!
—*Come Alive Program Greater Five Towns YM & YWHA*

The program for each individual student with disabilities is called an Individualized Education Program (IEP). Until I did something about it, teachers only had access to each student's IEP and were not provided with a copy of the document. How is it possible to have a program tailored to a student with a disability and not give his or providers a copy of the plan? After writing and securing passage of a law that rectified this situation, I said, "It is absurd that teachers, who are frequently required to simultaneously implement several programs for several students with varying and diverse disabilities, were not provided with a copy of the program itself. This new law will maximize the ability of our teaching professionals to carry out these programs and will go a long way toward improving compliance with existing laws."

The law also required, for the first time, bus drivers and other school employees working with the student to be informed of the provisions in the IEP relevant to their interaction with the student. This common-sense information sharing measure has done much to improve the services special children receive in school.

In October, I gave an emotional speech at the Long Beach Chamber in support of the United States Army Corps of Engineers Storm Damage Reduction Project, where I voiced my concern about what I believed was the imminent (a relative term, when one speaks about the weather) danger to our barrier island from future storms. The Council was to decide whether or not to participate in the $85 million proposed beach project.

As then-Councilman Lenny Remo said, "There is no stronger advocate for the people and the environment in Long Beach than Assemblyman Weisenberg. He speaks with his heart and his years of legislative experience when discussing the Army Corps project."

While not everyone agreed with my recommendation, I believe that time has proven my concerns warranted.

In November, I joined with the staff and young members of the South Shore YJCC, then Executive Vice President Arnie Preminger, as well as the Jewish War Veterans of Long Beach, in dedicating a flag pole outside the Oceanside YJCC in honor of Hy Goldstein of Long Beach, who was a volunteer pilot and an honorary colonel in the Israeli military. Hy Goldstein was an amazing, courageous gentleman who flew a beat-up propeller plane on Israel's behalf in 1947, close to an enemy plane, and because he had no artillery, lit a pipe bomb and was about to throw it at the enemy, when he dropped the bomb between his legs in the cockpit. With too little time to fumble around for it, this quick-thinking pilot—and dear friend—flipped the plane upside down, causing the bomb to drop onto the enemy aircraft. The FBI was tasked with enforcing the post-war arms embargo, and they were after Hy and other American heroes for their active military support of Israel. Undeterred, undermanned, and outgunned, Hy Goldstein and other brave men took on Egyptian spitfires. So I made sure we dedicated that flagpole to my friend, and Israel's friend, Hy Goldstein, a true hero.

Also that month, I was re-elected for my seventh term, and was quoted in the newspaper as saying, "I want to help people get quality of life, dignity, health care, and help them protect our environment, as well as help our children."

Just after the election, I received the following from a pretty prominent Republican at the State level: "'Way to go! Congratulations on a job well done. My sincere best wishes to you and your family, and if there is ever anything I can do to assist you or your staff, please do not hesitate to call. Keep up the good work." And there was a handwritten note that read: "Love to Ellen! Regards, George." From my friend, Governor Pataki, of course.

The year 2002 culminated in my being named "Legislator of the Year" by the New York State American Heart Association, because of my efforts to enact legislation ensuring that every school in the state is equipped with an automated external defibrillator (AED). To this day, people still tell me that these are continuing to save lives.

2003—A New Role

I was honored to be appointed Assistant Speaker Pro Tempore, a majority leadership position, by Assembly Speaker Sheldon Silver, a position I carried out with diligence and enthusiasm. This meant that in the absence of the Speaker, along with the Speaker Pro Tempore, I would preside over the Legislative Session and oversee the parliamentary procedures of the house while legislation is debated and acted upon. It was an honor to be named to this role.

This year was in a very real sense, the year of working with health care. I was able to help a number of organizations in our communities each obtain $50,000 through the Community Capital Assistance Program for improvements and expansions of their facilities. Long Beach Medical Center used this money to upgrade and refurbish its outdated Ambulatory Surgery Unit.

Nassau University Medical Center used their grant to relocate their Eye Center from a temporary trailer in a parking lot to a proper medical facility on their grounds, improving accessibility, enhancing services, and allowing for the treatment of more patients.

South Nassau Hospital was able to expand their Emergency Services Department to accommodate more patients.

The AHRC of Nassau (which stands for Association for the Help of Retarded Children) was able to upgrade and renovate its Camp Loyaltown, a sleepaway camp in the Catskills that gives children and adults the opportunity to participate in recreational and social activities.

United Cerebral Palsy (UCP) of Nassau County was able to expand primary care services to individuals with developmental disabilities and traumatic brain injury.

Last, but certainly not least, the Long Beach City School District was able to pay for a safety and security communications upgrade, which improved district-wide communications, especially on snow days and during emergency conditions.

We built upon the wonderful success of our Coats for Kids program, as our community donated more than three thousand coats for the needy—a new record! Helpful organizations included the local Daisies, Brownies, and Girl Scouts, and clergy. This organization was such a two-way street. We helped people who might not have had coats to stay warm, and we gave young people the opportunity to help others. There is no greater reward. I'm sure this was the start, or perhaps the continuation, of giving for many of these kids, who probably went on to do still more good work down the road.

This one's a biggie for Long Beach, and in areas that means so much to me, fitness and water sports. I was able to secure a $500,000 grant from the New York State Dormitory Authority for major renovations to the Recreation Center on Magnolia Boulevard. The heating and ventilation system was replaced, a lift was added to provide accessibility to the pool for those with physical challenges, and repairs were made to the roof and the north wall of the swimming pool.

In February, our city lost one of the pillars of Long Beach when Ed Buscemi passed away. Former Council President, All-American baseball player, and "cop's cop;" one of the best police commissioners the city has ever seen, as his daughter, Laurie remembered him. To me, Ed was a lifelong friend, fellow lifeguard, and police colleague who joined the police force in Long Beach the exact same day I did. Ed moved here from the Bronx with his widowed mother in 1945, having spent many summers here in the family's place on Ocean View. After serving sixteen years on the police force, Ed then served as commissioner. Following his retirement in 1976, he was anxious to get "back into action," according to Larry Elovich, then president of the Long Beach Chamber of Commerce (who passed away in 2012). Talk about action. Ed served on the Zoning Board of Appeals, and in 1988, began his thirteen-year tenure on the City Council, while serving as unpaid Executive Director of the Chamber, a post he held for seventeen years, until his death. They just don't make them like Ed Buscemi anymore. I still miss him.

The chaplain in Albany who often opened the sessions was a priest named Father Peter Young, who came to me and said that he had been Ed's roommate at Sienna College, and Ed was such a great baseball player that "he never had to steal second base . . . because he always hit the ball out of the park." He was loved and respected by everyone.

In 2003, Ellen and I inaugurated a new annual tradition called "A Labor of Love," a special award that would be a tribute to organized labor and would, each year, benefit organizations dedicated to serving the needs of people with disabilities. The awards were named for Ricky and given specifically to people who serve the needs of others, people who help people, and it took the form of beautiful sculptures created by the artist Richard Kramer. Each award came with a card inscribed with the following poem written by Mr. Kramer.

Mentor
When no one noticed
You saw me struggling
You could have passed but didn't
Your thinking and your smiles convinced me to excel

Your steadfast faith in me compelled me to succeed.
And if by chance I didn't you'd still be there for me.
It is good to have someone like you.
—Richard Kramer

We gave out the Ricky awards later in the year.

This was also the year I dedicated a therapeutic horseback riding center in honor of my friend, the late Assemblyman Jacob Gunther of Sullivan County. An outstanding legislator who was deeply admired by his colleagues and much loved by his family and many friends, Jake passed away in the summer of 2003. The Jacob Gunther Therapeutic Horseback Riding Center is part of Jened Recreation Village in Rock Hill in Sullivan, and is owned and operated by Cerebral Palsy Associations of New York State. This beautiful center features a horse barn, corral, and petting zoo. It brought a lot of smiles to a lot of faces.

On July 1, the roads all over New York State became a little bit safer when we established a new, higher standard for identifying those driving while intoxicated. I was a prime sponsor of the law that lowered legal blood alcohol concentration (BAC) from .10 to .08 percent, sending a clear message that New York does not tolerate mixing alcohol and driving. In 2003, alcohol-related auto accidents killed one American every twenty minutes, according to the U.S. Department of Transportation. We established higher standards not only for driving, but also for boating and snowmobiling, all of which saved lives.

We may occasionally take our relationship with our doctors for granted, but we put enormous trust in our doctors. It's a given. In 2003, I was appalled to read about a pediatric neurosurgeon in the Albany area, Dr. Phillip Riback, who had been arrested and charged with sexually abusing a number of his young patients. The sense of betrayal and devastation experienced by these children and their families must have been horrible. To make matters worse, the New York State Department of Health was not, at that time, required to report such behavior to law enforcement officials. It was revealed that the Department of Health had received several complaints about this predator and spent years investigating—during which more children were molested. Their investigation consisted of an administrative review by their Board of Professional Medical Conduct, which is a secretive process and takes years. Meanwhile, new patients were seeing Dr. Riback at this time and had no idea what was happening. The nature of the typical patient in this practice made them vulnerable to abuse, and the medical community protected its own at the expense of unsuspecting children and families who were in need of pediatric neurological care. No criminal charges were brought against this doctor until one parent called the police (not the Health Department) directly.

I quickly wrote legislation to halt this deplorable practice, which was signed into law by my friend, Governor George Pataki. The new law requires Health Department officials to report any suspected criminal activity by a physician to the appropriate district attorney's office. The neurosurgeon was convicted in 2014 on multiple charges. Dr. Riback was sentenced to forty-eight years in prison, served five years, won an appeal on a technicality, and was set free in 2011. He did lose his license to practice medicine and cannot reapply for it. My bill didn't have anything to do with the appeal, but it changed the way future complaints to the Department of Health are handled. It hasn't stopped other sexual predators from harming children, but if there were a way I could do so, I certainly would.

The Governor also signed into law a bill I introduced to protect cancer survivors from being unfairly discriminated against when applying for or renewing life insurance or non-cancellable disability insurance. The law ensured, as I said in my newsletter, "that New Yorkers who have suffered from cancer will not be denied access to the insurance coverage they need to protect themselves and their families."

Close to ninety-thousand New Yorkers were diagnosed with cancer in 2003. Ensuring that these people would not be denied vital insurance would, I'm certain, be of some comfort to individuals and families already burdened with challenging circumstances.

Amazing Project Challenge honored my beloved Ellen as one of its "Wind Beneath My Wings" award recipients of 2003. The event program noted that Ellen was the wife of "our most dedicated Assemblyman, Harvey Weisenberg," and that she graduated from Great Neck High School and Adelphi University's School of Nursing. She worked, the program explained, for Long Beach Hospital and the Bayview Nursing Home, and was also a school nurse and a private duty nurse. The program noted that Ellen had long been active in organizations, including AHRC and the Juvenile Diabetes Research Foundation. Her favorite activities included boardwalk walking, cooking, and baking, working in her garden, swimming, and reading. Her most important role, the program explained, was being my wife, and accompanying me to Albany, and sharing my problems and easing the pain associated with my work. I tell you this so you will see how God has blessed me with this wonderful saint.

In June, we were able to expand on the work begun three years earlier with Bob Policastro and Walter Stockton of IGHLP, by building a second Angela's House facility in Smithtown to house and care for medically fragile children close to home. I involved public officials from both parties, and secured $500,000 towards its construction.

Also in 2003, Ellen and I were proud to be honored by Long Beach Medical Center at their eighty-first anniversary Autumn Ball. Now, while that was nice, I am perhaps even prouder of another dinner that year, held in October in Lido Beach, that benefited two camps for people with disabilities: AHRC's Camp Loyaltown and UCP's Camp Jened. We brought together much of Long Island's community of support, for that's what it was, for people with developmental disabilities. That's where Ellen and I surprised special guests by giving out our Ricky awards to unsuspecting attendees.

We saw their expressions of surprise and delight and heard them say things like, "I can't believe Harvey's giving me an award." That was said by Bob Policastro of Angela's House. Similar reactions were shared by: Mike Mascari of AHRC; Bob McGuire of UCP; Jim Conlon of CURB; Paul Cullen of Camp Loyaltown; Stephanie Kahn of the SJK Foundation (which provides listening therapy to aid in the healing process for people in hospitals, nursing homes, adult centers, and schools); Tom Maul of Office of Mental Retardation and Developmental Disabilities; special education teachers Doris Jones and Donna Caldera; Blanch Fierstein of the AHRC, *Able* magazine publisher Angela Melledy; and of course, Walter Stockton of IGHLP.

"It was a night of love with wonderful people," I said that night, "who all share a common interest in providing quality care, dignity, and respect for all people who have differences."

I passed a bill, which Governor Pataki signed into law, further protecting our people with developmental disabilities, by requiring that new and prospective caregivers be fingerprinted. This would give licensed facilities access to any criminal histories employees or prospective employees might have, and, of course, prevent potential abuse.

I was able to directly help students in Oceanside with a $150,000 grant, which paid for mobile laptop setups for science and math research at the middle school; expanded video conferencing throughout the district; Regents preparation and tutoring; and a Best Buddies program, which allowed students with disabilities to access the Internet to stay in touch with friends at remote locations, and introduce students with disabilities to the business world. Money well spent!

2004—Water Preservation

Our beach is a delicate ecosystem, but so is our water supply, the Lloyd aquifer, said by scientists to be the oldest, deepest, and probably purest source of water on Long Island. In early 2004, New York City wanted to pump overflow water from the upstate Delaware and Catskill aquifers into our Lloyd aquifer to be stored and, in the event of emergency, used by the City. "I just don't want people playing in our Lloyd," I said at a hearing on the issue in early 2004. "You can swim in our ocean, but don't take our water." I meant what I said, and the upshot was, no one messed with our Lloyd.

In 2004, I secured a grant to renovate the athletic field at Lindell School where I had long ago been a student athlete. Several community constituency groups made up the committee that provided recommendations, and the result was a multi-purpose athletic field, for soccer and lacrosse, and a second field to be used primarily for softball. The facilities were to be shared by the Long Beach PAL, Lacrosse, CYO Soccer, Long Beach Little League, and the Long Beach Recreational Center. The fields were also to be used by the Long Beach Middle School athletic programs as well as the Physical Education Department of Lindell School. I am proud to have been instrumental in providing the funds for this worthwhile endeavor, and was deeply moved by the ceremony in July, dedicating the field in my honor. Participating in the ceremony were Superintendent of Schools Ron Friedman, Board of Education President Patrick Gallagher, Long Beach Director of Athletics Arnold Epstein, Lindell Principal Karen Sauter, former New York Jet Marty Lyons, and quite a few student athletes.

I secured a $50,000 grant for Nassau University Medical Center to acquire a high-tech camera to better serve people with potentially serious vision problems. The camera, which might not have been affordable for the "cash-strapped" hospital, according to newspaper reports at the time, would allow images of the retina to instantly be sent to computers, allowing for potentially faster diagnoses, especially for people with diabetes.

I dedicated my 2004 newsletter to my Ellen and the words with which I did so I must repeat to you, because they remain an accurate reflection of my feelings even now, many years later. "Ellen's insights and intellect are invaluable to me," I wrote. "But it is her grace, her humanity, and her boundless compassion that never fail to fill my heart. The maneuvering of Albany can leave me uncertain of many things, but of this I am certain: I am a better person because of Ellen." So true.

In August, CURB founder James Conlon passed away at the age of sixty-four. He was my friend of twenty-five years. We had worked together on many projects in Long Beach, and as a result, there were now handicapped-accessible ramps to our boardwalk, beach wheelchairs, curb cuts, handicapped parking, lifts, and elevators. He knew what it was like to be in a chair, and what it was like to need help. The loss of his spirit was a big one to all of us. The late Jim Monahan remembered James as "always so positive about everything," and credited Conlon with helping him realize that life in a wheelchair wasn't so bad. Jim Conlon was an upbeat, can-do guy, and such an inspiration. We worked together to make the beach more accessible for people with disabilities. He truly was an ambassador for the disabled. The reconstruction of Ocean View in the West End was dedicated in his honor. Ocean View has since been renamed Jim Conlon Way.

In September, Long Beach held our first surfing program for children with autism. As a lifeguard and an examiner for Long Beach for so long, I have witnessed the joy and excitement of youngsters with disabilities experiencing in the ocean, a joy their families may not have thought possible. Years before, I had met former world champion surfer Izzy Paskowitz. When Izzy's son Isaiah, who is autistic, learned to surf, he enjoyed it immensely. As a result, Paskowitz founded the Surfer's Healing Foundation, an organization dedicated to spreading the positive powers of surfing.

I told Izzy that I would commit to hosting a surfing for kids with disabilities program in Long Beach, along with Jim Mulvaney, a Pulitzer-prize winning journalist and the father of an autistic son, Danny, who at seventeen learned to surf from Paskowitz in Rockaway. The first year we had over a hundred participants. In order for the program to be successful, I involved the Long Beach Recreation Department, the Beach Maintenance Department, the Long Beach Lifeguards, and the Sanitation Department, and arranged for food and drinks to be available for everyone.

To see the pleasure and enjoyment on the faces of these young people who were loving this new experience was so amazing. Watching the parents take such pleasure in witnessing their children doing something they had thought utterly impossible, and loving it, may have been the most rewarding of all. I spent the whole day in the ocean participating, being happy to be a part of their joy.

I remember a girl of about twelve or thirteen on the beach who could not walk. I carried her in my own arms to a surfboard and watched her on that surfboard, riding her first wave, in the arms of one of our instructors. I saw an expression I will never forget, true boundless joy.

The year ended with yet another election, and I secured my eighth term. I also earned a lot of criticism for backing Republican Dean Skelos over his Democratic opponent Joshua Ketover. This was just one of the many ways I got myself into trouble. But I believed supporting Skelos was the best way to get the things from our Senate we needed for our region. It's better than having another person in there without the authority to get things done. I was just being honest. I also urged all political parties to work together, stating: "You only have progress when everyone works together." I work with whoever is there; the powers that be. I will cross party lines to be able to do whatever is best for my constituents.

2005—Water Quality and Preparedness

The year began with an article in *Newsday* in which I got both praise and criticism for my work on behalf of special needs children. One person said that my work on behalf of the disabled may distract me from using my political collateral to take on broader issues in Albany. Others called me a blessed person for helping their family member. Look, some people don't understand what families have to deal with when they have a special needs child. In 2005, Ricky was forty-seven years old, and Ellen and I still had to change his diapers. But he always made us smile. It has always mattered to me to focus more on what children can do, not what they can't.

Besides, the criticism wasn't warranted as by then I had sponsored more than two hundred bills that had become law, including tax relief, education, health care, and law enforcement. I didn't focus on politics. I focused on helping people in need. That's what politics means to me, and the reality is that people miss what's really important.

You know what's great, and I'm sure you'll agree? Getting paid in advance. Right? Well in 2005, through what's called a "'spin-up" of New York State revenue funds, I was able to help secure, with the help of then State Senator Dean Skelos, $700,000 in funds designated for our city a year earlier than anticipated. So Long Beach received nearly $750,000, a year ahead of schedule. Not bad!

I hosted a Valentine's Brunch to benefit children with special needs, a day I shared with, then, New York State Attorney General Eliot Spitzer, who was my guest of honor. The event was truly a bipartisan one, as it was also attended by Republicans Al D'Amato and State Senator Dean Skelos, as well as dignitaries from both sides of the aisle. What was the most important aspect of that day? The money we raised from this and an earlier, similar event which then went to AHRC, Angela's House II, Nassau UCP, the Best Buddies Program (dedicated to ending the social, physical, and economic isolation of people with intellectual and developmental disabilities), and the Long Island Toy Lending Center, started by Colleen Moseman, which loans adaptive toys to severely disabled children.

Once again, the terrific Coats for Kids program brought out the best in our community, as our wonderful residents demonstrated typical generosity and compassion and we were able to distribute more than sixty-five hundred coats to needy children and adults. That was ten thousand coats in three years! Our schools, the Brownies, and our community organizations all joined together. The dry cleaners cleaned the coats for free, and my terrific staff spent countless hours picking up and sorting coats, getting them to and from the cleaners, and making sure that each recipient received the right coat. Gives you a warm feeling, doesn't it?

Some stories are simply heartbreaking. They are more than stories. The people behind the stories became part of the fabric of my life, as I became a part of the fabric of theirs when I was able to help them. At nine every morning, a mother named Rachel Amar would drive an hour and a half from Hewlett, Long Island to Westchester. Why? To be with her two-year-old son, Max, who suffered brain stem atrophy at birth and required a ventilator to breathe. The problem was that Long Island had no ventilators for children, hence the long, daily drive. To make matters worse, the Westchester facility requested that Max be moved to New Jersey.

So you can see why one of my great passions has been to provide long-term pediatric facilities so that families like the Amars can live with as great a quality of life as possible. I made it my business to lobby our State government for exactly that, "to make sure we get a facility that's going to provide for this child and others in our region," I was quoted as saying at the time. Max was eventually placed in a facility close to home.

I had the extraordinary honor of being the first recipient of *Spectrum* magazine's Harvey Weisenberg Lifetime Achievement Award. *Spectrum* offered a central place for resources and idea exchange for parents, teachers, therapists, and other professionals involved with autism spectrum disorder. It filled a real need for the many, many parents who are struggling to understand their child's autism diagnosis and the vast array of treatments and resources available to them. It was quite an honor!

Because of the huge growth in the number of children diagnosed with autism and related disorders, I passed a resolution making April "Autism Awareness Month" and spoke at the Long Island Autism Awareness Day Fair, which was attended by more than eight-hundred people.

Ellen and I were pleased and excited to join legendary singer-songwriter James Taylor at his Jones Beach performance, which helped raise money to place lifesaving AEDs in schools across the country.

I was also pleased to attend Governor Pataki's Prayer Breakfast, attended by many hundreds of people, where the talented Brittany Maier performed. Though blind and autistic, Brittany, who was sixteen at that time, is a gifted pianist and musical savant who still performs around the country. This young lady can play any song she hears or has ever heard on the piano. What an incredible gift.

You know the saying "sticks and stones. . ."? I don't necessarily agree. People with disabilities are frequently referred to by the fact that they have a disability, rather than as people first. Terms like "autistic boy" or "wheelchair-bound individual" have always bothered me. So

I did something about it. I introduced a bill, which became law, mandating state publications to refer to people before their disability or limitation. It's a simple matter of respect and people-first language.

Mercury is a known neurotoxin and has long been identified as injurious to the brain. By banning mercury from vaccines and immunizations, we could protect future generations of children from exposure to this harmful neurotoxin. So I authored a bill that did exactly that; it prohibited the administration of any vaccination or immunization containing thimerosal, which is fifty percent mercury, or any mercury-based additives, preservatives, or disinfectants to children or pregnant women.

Do you have any idea how many 911 calls are made from cell phones? A lot! I was able to provide a grant of $3.4 million to help upgrade enhanced 911 systems for Nassau County, including life-saving, location tracing technology. I also secured $50,000 to enable the Long Beach Police Department to substantially improve its aging communications system.

Unfortunately, all too often, it takes a tragedy for necessary change to be brought about. Amy Plantz was a mother who went looking for her sixteen-year-old son Chris one evening when he failed to return home on his bicycle. She found Chris by the side of the road, the victim of a vehicular hit-and-run. Her son was still alive, but had been left to die in a roadside ditch by the drunk driver who hit him. He died the next day from his injuries.

At that time, penalties for leaving the scene of an accident were much less than a DWI. This anomaly in law came about due to incremental increases in penalties for DWI over the years, while leaving the scene penalties remained level. This created a dangerous incentive for drunk drivers to flee the scene, rather than seek medical attention for their victims. I wrote legislation that brought hit-and-run penalties to more appropriate levels. When the bill became law, Chris's mother Amy said, "One of the most cowardly acts is to leave someone to die. My son could have been saved if help had gotten to him sooner. I am grateful to have this legislation as his legacy."

In the summer, the Friedberg Jewish Community Center in Oceanside partnered with the Henry Kaufmann Campgrounds, which is in Wheatley Heights on the Nassau-Suffolk border, to open the first and only day camp in New York State for children suffering from cancer or cancer-related disorders. Sunrise Day Camp made it possible for children with cancer to enjoy a summer of fun, friendship, and activities—things that are often denied them because of their medical conditions. I was honored to be asked to serve as the honorary chair of this worthy cause, for which I raised nearly a million dollars.

"Assemblyman Weisenberg's involvement with Sunrise Day Camp should come as no surprise to anyone, as no one champions the cause of people with disabilities and chronic illnesses as fiercely and passionately as he has," said Arnie Preminger, then Executive Vice President of the Friedberg JCC. "His acceptance of the position of Honorary Chair of Sunrise Day Camp is anything but honorary; he has accepted this position so as to be able to advocate on our behalf and to draw attention to the needs of these unique children and the critically important work which the camp has set out to do."

Not only do these children with such devastating conditions go to this wonderful camp, but their brothers and sisters can as well. Since its inception, Camp Sunrise has expanded to be a year-round program that now also serves children in Israel.

In September, I obtained a $50,000 grant to assist Father Thomas Donohoe's St. Mary of the Isle Parish in obtaining a new roof for their facility. But the State Dormitory Authority refused to pay for a roof over the sanctuary, as this would mean state funds would be paying for a religious structure. So I said, "Let's evaluate the needs of the church and community center." I was told that an oil burner would be needed in the community center, which is not religious in nature. Sometimes navigating our system and finding ways to help communities takes a little creativity. We got Father Tom's people an oil burner.

In late October, on the heels of Hurricane Katrina, I hosted a gathering in the sixth-floor auditorium of City Hall that brought together residents from multiple South Shore beach communities to discuss how to meet the threat posed by potential hurricanes. "We're going to get hit," I told the audience. "It's just a matter of time." How would an evacuation of forty-eight-thousand people be possible, with so few gas stations and evacuation routes? It would take a minimum of two days, in advance of the event, preferably three. Of further concern is the fact that two of our evacuation routes, the Meadowbrook Parkway and Austin Boulevard, are themselves prone to flooding.

Together with a thirteen-person panel, I led a discussion. Our meeting took place during a period of a record number of hurricanes in the Atlantic Ocean and major rains. How would the Nassau Expressway, Route 878, fare when packed with tens of thousands of cars fleeing an oncoming category one or two hurricane? "No one is safe on the barrier beach," I told the people.

One solution I was determined to pursue and did in fact get done was to raise some of our most vulnerable roadways along the evacuation route. A second solution was to build dunes, and I have never been shy about looking people right in the eye and telling them that a potentially unpopular solution is exactly what is needed. "If this means our beaches won't be as beautiful," I said publicly at the time, "then so be it."

Speaking of water, I helped to bring more than $9 million in grants to our communities to "improve water quality and protect and restore habitats" throughout our South Shore estuaries. The grants were funded through the Clean Water/Clean Air Bond Act and the Environmental Protection Fund, and supported projects to reduce pollutants from entering the estuary through storm water and runoff, and to restore habitats and install fish ladders to allow for upstream spawning.

Right around that time, I received a lovely thank you from George and Libby Pataki for attending their prayer breakfast and helping to make it a success.

I acquired a $100,000 grant for AHRC's Camp Loyaltown to help upgrade their electrical system. Modernizing facilities such as theirs goes a long way toward providing quality services.

I was honored to be a featured speaker in early November 2005 at NYSARCs 56th Annual Convention at Kutsher's Country Club in Monticello.

A situation was brought to my attention about a young man with a developmental disability, Jesse Greenfield, who was a resident at an AHRC facility for more than twenty-nine years. Jesse had fainted and was rushed to the hospital, but, because he was unable to understand what was happening, resisted, struggled, and ultimately was physically restrained by having his wrists tied to his gurney. The AHRC nurse, who had traveled with him to the hospital, was refused entry. Jesse's parents, also, were denied entry.

When I learned of this, I was able to introduce and pass a bill with Assemblyman Tom DiNapoli that gave everyone with developmental disabilities the right to have a loved one or advocate present at their hospital bed. The bill passed unanimously into New York State law. Although Jesse passed away in May 2004 from an unrelated illness, his suffering brought about change that helps others.

"This bill is Jesse's legacy," said his mother. "And I was so pleased that there is now a law, and we have rights and it includes everyone who is nonverbal and everyone who can't speak." Jesse's difficult situation, along with his family's and my advocacy doubtlessly saved lives.

2006—Point Lookout

By 2006 I had spent thirty years in public service. I was deeply honored when the Governor and representatives from all walks of Long Island and New York State life, from the many nonprofit organizations I have been blessed to work alongside, to firefighters from right here in Atlantic Beach, honored my thirty years of public service at a humbling event at the Sands in Atlantic Beach.

In February, there was a private effort to build a Liquified Natural Gas (LNG) facility off our beach. This is when the gloves come off. "If God wanted another island south of Long Beach, he would have put it there!" I said, in a phone call from the floor of the Assembly. No island! No LNG!

As both a former police officer and as a citizen, I have always supported tough measures on crime and keeping our people safe. In 2006, my colleagues in the Assembly and I overwhelmingly approved a DNA databank expansion legislation that roughly tripled the size of New York's DNA database. It encompassed all persons convicted of felonies and eighteen key misdemeanors that involve violence, threats of violence, menacing, or stalking behavior, or offenses against children. We also approved a measure to eliminate the criminal statute of limitations for felony rape cases and extend the civil statute of limitations in these cases from one year to five years, so that the victims of these heinous crimes have every possible opportunity to seek justice. We extended the authority to prosecute and to bring civil action for a range of sexual crimes.

Rape is a horrific crime that leaves a lifelong emotional scar. It is wrong to limit the ability of victims of sexual predators to bring their attackers to justice. We also imposed up-to-life sentences for the most heinous sex crimes. In addition, those convicted of the new crimes of predatory sexual assault, and predatory sexual assault against a child, were hereafter required to register under the Sexual Offender Registration Act (SORA), known as Megan's Law. New York had enacted Megan's Law in 1995, and it was signed by Governor Pataki. Under Megan's Law—named for seven-year-old Megan Kanka of California, who was raped and murdered by a known child molester—sex offenders are required to register with the state after conviction, or if they serve time in prison, upon their release, and notify the registry when they relocate. Sex offenders who move to New York from another state also must register.

Several other states enacted the same laws and it became a federal law that was passed by President Bill Clinton in 1996. In 2006, the goal of the Sexual Offender Registration Act was to close potential gaps and loopholes that existed under prior law and strengthen the nationwide network of sex offender registration and notification programs. SORA established a Sex Offender Registry within the New York State Division of Criminal Justice Services.

I had the honor in 2006 of inviting Senator Hillary Rodham Clinton to accept the Nassau County AHRC's Humanitarian of the Year award for her work and dedicated effort on behalf of others at the 2006 Rose Ball, which was attended by nearly one thousand people, including the wonderful Stephanie Joyce Kahn, founder of the Stephanie Joyce Kahn Foundation.

By year's end I had won my ninth term in the State Assembly. In other election news, Nassau County Executive Tom Suozzi ran in a Democratic primary for governor in 2006 against Attorney General Eliot Spitzer, whom I supported and who ultimately won. Somehow, the public, or at least some newspaper writers, thought I had what they referred to as "an icy" relationship with Suozzi. Not true! "I don't dislike this kid," I said of Suozzi, who was forty-three at the time. "I support him as County Executive, and have since he took office in any and every way I could. But I have to consider who is best qualified. With Eliot Spitzer being successful, the Assembly Democrats will have a partner to work with, which we haven't had in twelve years. Now Suozzi presents an adversarial position to the Legislature," I explained. "You can never quote Tom Suozzi saying something bad about me. This is a perception that people generate themselves. It's not real. . . .. I've worked very hard to help Tom Suozzi be successful."

2007—Jonathan's Law

Jonathan Carey's story remains one of the most heartbreaking issues I have ever encountered in all of my years of public service. Jonathan was a little boy with autism who was abused, then later killed, by a system that was supposed to protect and care for him.

In the waning June days of the legislative session of 2006, Lisa and Michael Carey walked into my Albany office seeking assistance. As upstate New York residents, the Careys were not my constituents. They had made several attempts to see their own legislators and others, but said they had not received a response or help from the any of their representatives in Albany. My staff and I welcomed them and listened while Lisa and Michael told me that eleven-year-old Jonathan was born with severe developmental disabilities, first diagnosed as "retarded," then later with autism.

While they were able to care for Jonathan at home for many years, by the time he was nine, they knew he needed care that went beyond what they were humanly capable of. Jonathan was nonverbal and, by all accounts, was functioning at a two-year-old level; he needed diapers and constant supervision to keep him safe. At the recommendation of the "experts," Jonathan was placed at the Anderson Center for Autism in Dutchess County, a private residential school that specialized in the field of autism.

After living at Anderson for a time, Jonathan began losing weight. The Careys became concerned and their instincts were telling them something was wrong. One day, the parents visited to take Jonathan for a medical appointment. As they left, an employee handed them a backpack and seemed to be encouraging them to look inside the bag. When they did, they found records of Jonathan's "care" at Anderson School. I remember being sickened when I read details of numerous instances of food being withheld from Jonathan because he took his shirt off or some other "infraction." When withheld food did not prove to be effective at modifying Jonathan's behavior, the school added isolation to the starvation. Jonathan missed at least eight full days of school, locked alone in his room, with paper covering the windows to prevent him from looking outside or seeing the daylight. Keep in mind that he was just eleven years old.

The fact that this was happening nearly forty-five years after Ellen discovered Ricky's horrific state in an upstate facility was heart-break-ing to both of us. How could this still be occurring in our state and in our country? The Careys had come to the right person to understand their fears and concerns.

Some alarming realities were immediately apparent to me. The so-called behavior modifications inflicted on Jonathan were considered to be "aversive therapy," a practice outlawed in New York. The school district that placed Jonathan in Anderson School sent him there with a completed Individual Education Program and a Behavior Interven-tion Plan. Neither of these documents, of course, dictated this abuse. Reading further, we discovered that Jonathan's behavior plan was changed by an individual at the Anderson School without a Committee on Special Education (CSE) meeting to review and discuss his progress and to make plans for the coming year, which should have included Jonathan's school district and his parents. But, most disturbing of all, no criminal charges had been brought against the perpetrators of this ille-gal activity, despite the fact that the Careys had reported it to everyone who could possibly be in a position to do something.

The district attorney in that jurisdiction claimed they had investi-gated, but did not have sufficient evidence to bring charges. Although every abuse inflicted on Jonathan was well documented by the school, law enforcement failed Jonathan and all the other victims at Anderson.

The legislature was prepared to conclude session for the year. We needed time to read through piles of records fought for and given to us by Jonathan's family. I met with Assembly lawyers to grapple with how to proceed. Was a new law necessary when these things were already illegal? Should we try enforcement or reporting? Should we increase penalties for the crime itself or for not reporting? Can the Legislature compel a district attorney to act sensibly? How? Were other district attorneys lacking in this area or was this an isolated lapse? These were just a few of the ingredients necessary to craft a law that would not only gain the support of enough legislators to be approved, but would also effectively protect children in the future by deterring more bad acts.

Throughout that summer and fall, I worked with Legislative law-yers to come up with solutions. The Careys, of course, had removed Jon-athan from the Anderson School. The state investigated and produced a report that was more than four-hundred pages long. The Careys requested a copy of the report and used every legal method available to obtain it. Each and every request was denied. The Careys were finally given a brief, one-page summary of that report.

At that point, we all concurred that withholding these investigative records was a travesty and allowed the status-quo to quietly continue. The public sector needs transparency and this climate of secrecy became my focus for reform. We began drafting a bill that amended the Mental Hygiene Law by requiring parental notification within twenty-four hours of injuries or incidents of abuse or neglect. Further, the bill was very clear that parents and guardians are entitled to investigative reports and other records about their loved ones that could no longer be withheld. I was encouraged by the possibility of forging a new path; if agencies were unwilling to report these incidents to law enforcement, then we could, through this legislation, allow parents to report the crimes themselves by equipping them with the necessary information to do so.

So Jonathan's Law was drafted, introduced, and ready by the beginning of the new session in January 2007. The bill was referred to the Assembly's Mental Health Committee. I began negotiations with the committee and Assembly leadership to get the bill moving for a committee and floor vote, while also asking several senators to introduce my bill in their house. These are all necessary steps to get a law passed, even a no-brainer like this one.

Throughout January and February, the legislature is typically focused on budget formation, negotiation, and passage. Bills like Jonathan's Law are usually done post-budget, but that never stopped me from trying. The Careys had enrolled Jonathan in O.D. Heck, a state-operated facility that was closer to the Careys home, which enabled them to visit frequently.

Jonathan was still suffering from the after-effects of being starved and abused. The damage done to him at Anderson School manifested itself in physical outbursts and he was somewhat more difficult to manage. Being nonverbal, there was no other way for Jonathan to express the trauma he had experienced. At OD Heck, there were at least three incidents of unexplained bruising and injuries that were severe enough to require medical attention. Again, the Careys were never given details on how the injuries occurred.

The Legislature recesses every February during President's week. Schools are closed, and it's a quiet time when many head to warmer climates or skiing vacations. With session concluded for a week, Ellen and I left for Florida. The next day, February 16, we received the news that Jonathan Carey had been killed the previous evening, suffocated by a direct caregiver who used an illegal restraint on him while on an outing to the local mall. This news was so devastating for Ellen and me, hitting close to home, and striking fear into the hearts of every parent who had no choice in placing their vulnerable child into the care of an institution. We cried and grieved for this child who was lost, a casualty of a system that should have protected him instead.

While we mourned Jonathan, my Assembly office in Albany was being inundated with media inquiries. A spokesperson for the Carey family had mentioned the family was working with me on legislation stemming from Jonathan's earlier abuse at the Anderson School. Some awful facts were being uncovered by the police; Jonathan's death was due to an illegal restraint and arrests had been made.

It was learned that the two direct caregivers who were with Jonathan drove around doing personal errands for at least an hour after his death. This took place with a second resident in the van, another young boy who witnessed Jonathan's suffocation. This child was verbal enough and cognizant enough to give the police a statement of what he had witnessed.

Those who care for people with disabilities have a difficult job, and most are dedicated and hardworking. In young Jonathan's case, the worker ultimately judged by the system to have been responsible for his death, and sent to prison on manslaughter charges, had worked about two-hundred hours during the fifteen-day period prior to Jonathan's death. This worker's lack of judgment was undoubtedly exacerbated by exhaustion, which was avoidable, and which has yet to be prevented by our system of underpaid and overworked direct caregivers.

Once Jonathan's death became highly publicized, there was suddenly a great deal of interest in the issue. Within a week, the Senate, with much public fanfare and press conferences, wrote and passed their own bill, a slightly different version from mine. Yes, that means the people who refused to meet with the Careys passed legislation within hours of widespread media attention. This is a glimpse of partisan politics at its worse, and some of my greatest challenges came from having to gather the patience to work with people who I knew were not motivated by public service. Some of the same people who represented, but refused to help the Careys the previous year, had the audacity to contact my office demanding I do something!

Of course, I didn't let their lack of empathy or selfish motives win the day. I redoubled my efforts, rewrote my bill, and negotiated language everyone could live with. Despite his later career-ending actions, Governor Eliot Spitzer was an excellent help, and took a genuine personal interest in getting the bill passed. I am especially proud of Jonathan's Law, and only wish that this vitally important legislation had not come at such an awful price. Because politics can be personal, I had no way of knowing then that that very law would make it possible for Ellen and me to learn of abuse our own son Ricky was experiencing as an adult, a poignant and personal closed circle on a long-fought fight.

There is an important lesson to be learned from this, one we must never forget. Abuse is abuse, neglect is neglect, and a crime is a crime no matter where they occur. If a parent withheld food and locked their child in a room, missing school for eight days, they would be arrested and charged. We need to change how we think about abuse that occurs in institutions and schools. Abuse and any other crimes need to be directly reported to law enforcement. Don't count on the people in charge of an organization or institution to file those charges. Many of them are good people, but they have a built-in incentive to avoid negative publicity. These matters can be kept confidential within organizations. Crimes reported to the police, on the other hand, become public and brought into the light. And that, almost always, means the difference between action and inaction.

Though this was an emotional beginning to my work that year, there was an injection of light-heartedness between this and another tragedy that demanded our attention in Albany. In March, I passed a resolution that marked the month as Irish Heritage Month. This became an annual event, and I am proud I sponsored this resolution every year through 2014. Some of my colleagues joked that Irish Heritage Month was sponsored by a Jewish Assemblyman. Coincidentally, that same year, one of my colleagues who happened to be Irish, referred to me during a heated argument as "Assemblyman Weisenthal." I chuckled and said, "All us Irish guys look the same, right?" Later in that same hearing, another of my colleagues, also of Irish descent, referred to me correctly and quipped, "I'm one of those Irish guys that can pronounce Weisenberg."

In June, one of the most important pieces of legislation I have ever sponsored was as an outgrowth of a tragedy mourned by thirty-five thousand people here in Long Beach. In 2005, following a family wedding, a limousine carrying members of the Flynn and Tangney families on the Meadowbrook Parkway was struck head-on by a pickup truck driven the wrong way by a drunk driver, Martin Heidgen. Seven-year-old Katie Flynn, who had been a flower girl in her aunt's wedding only hours before, was killed, along with the limo driver, Stanley Rabinowitz. The pickup driver was convicted of murder, prosecuted by Nassau County District Attorney Kathleen Rice, and sentenced to eighteen years to life in prison.

So I sponsored a bill, along with Republican Senator Charles Fuschillo of Merrick. The bill created the crime of aggravated vehicular homicide, which may be charged when a death caused by drunken driving occurs along with other factors. These include an additional death or serious injury, a prior conviction of driving while intoxicated, a blood-alcohol level of 0.18 or higher, and driving with a suspended license.

I read a letter from little Katie's grandmother on the Assembly floor, just before the bill passed unanimously. "This is personal for me," I was quoted as saying. "It's an extension of my life and an extension of my community. It was a loss to the entire city of Long Beach." A loss, I must say, that is still deeply, deeply felt today.

The residents of Point Lookout will tell you that they sometimes feel like a forgotten community; not always, but now and then. So I made it my business to help to protect that beautiful community and its wonderful residents from the ravages of Mother Nature and the encroaching seas to the tune of $26 million in beach erosion projects. The first task? Dredging 700,000 cubic yards of sand from Jones Inlet onto Point Lookout and Lido Beach, itself a $7.6 million project. We brought together both sides of the aisle on this one. This was a project that was nixed by the City of Long Beach on the grounds that if sand were pumped from the ocean floor onto eroded parts of the beach, it would destroy its natural beauty. I did not agree. Ultimately this project led to the protection of these other neighboring beaches.

This was a bill that had to be signed by midnight on a particular date in July, so on the preceding day I drove up to Albany along with Ellen. I yelled at the Governor and his chief of staff, and was probably a pain to have to deal with. I'm not ordinarily one to raise my voice, but I do feel it is my responsibility to say what I feel because I believe the obligation of an elected official is to represent the voice of the people. And I am here to give them a voice and they have to hear my voice. In this case it worked because eventually I did receive a phone call at literally the eleventh hour, from Governor Spitzer, that he was going to sign this bill and would travel by helicopter for a joint press conference the next day. After the press conference, Governor Spitzer confided in me that he would not have signed the bill if I had not gone up there to make him aware of its importance.

I was able to secure $400,000 to help with the City's complete overhaul of the seven-hundred block of West Penn Street in front of Long Beach Catholic Regional School, work that improved the road, water, sewer, and sidewalk, and enhanced the entire area.

When Father Thomas Donohue of St. Mary of the Isle retired, I dedicated a bench in front of the church in his honor and as a thank you for his many years of service to the community. Ellen, Ricky, and I were photographed on the bench with Father Tom, who was a good friend.

This one will make you smile; it made a lot of people smile, especially on hot summer days. I secured a $100,000 state grant for a water park at Hudson Street and Rev. J. J. Evans Boulevard, dedicated to three life-long residents of Long Beach, all of whom were exceptional role models, as I mentioned earlier in the book.. Leroy Conyers and Sherman Brown were honored posthumously for their love and dedication to Long Beach, and Charlie Hassell, for whom the park was also named, was recognized for his outstanding contributions to our city.

In September, the Harvey Weisenberg Resource Center (HWRC) in Old Bethpage opened to welcome families from Long Island who have developmentally disabled family members. The HWRC was and is a full-service information location. If a parent or guardian calls after receiving a diagnosis for his or her child, the trained HWRC staff provides information and phone numbers to medical resources, counselors, and support groups.

It was named after me because of my many years of lobbying for special needs and children with autism. While I was flattered, I prefer to shine the light on the real heroes, the parents and workers who deliver the much-needed care to our special people. Besides, we had the star power of Oscar-nominated actress Cathy Moriarty at the opening, which left many in attendance star-struck.

Patrice Radowitz of Family Residence and Essential Enterprises (FREE), one of the nonprofit organizations partnering, along with Lifespire, Inc., to form the center, said, "This is a source that is so desperately needed. There's nothing like this in place." I'm so proud to be a part of this center, which was the very first of its kind.

When our bravest public servants, our firefighters, die in the line of duty, they deserve to be memorialized, whether they are paid or volunteer. So while attending a solemn ceremony honoring twelve fallen firefighters in Albany, I passed a note to Governor Spitzer, protesting the fact that two names from Long Island were not included on the New York State Fallen Firefighters Memorial. The note urged the Governor to intervene on behalf of volunteer firefighters Paul Brady and Wilbur Ritter, who died in August 2006. Brady of Malverne died when he was crushed while performing maintenance on a fire truck. Ritter of Sayville died of a heart attack while responding to an alarm.

"The fact that Mr. Ritter and Mr. Brady did not die while battling a blaze in no way diminishes their service, their heroic spirits or their willingness to place themselves in harm's way to protect others," I wrote in the letter. "The least we can do is provide this simple, but profound and enduring gesture of remembering them side by side with their brethren."

To see that this important symbolic tribute would be paid, going forward, I introduced a bill providing that firefighters who die in the line of duty have their names inscribed on our Albany memorial. "Wilbur Ritter and Paul Brady died protecting their fellow New Yorkers," I was quoted as saying at the time. "Denying the inclusion of names of firefighters who rightfully belong on the memorial is a travesty, and my bill would prevent it from ever happening again." It would take five more years before this was resolved.

We opened a second Harvey Weisenberg Resource Center in November 2007, this one at Lifespire, Gotham Plaza on 125th Street in Harlem, enabling the work of trained professionals to help our special people in New York City. "These Resource Centers will help devastated parents get what they need," I said, "to provide the best possible intervention and give their child the quality of life they are entitled to."

2008—Towing Issues

In March 2008 Governor Eliot Spitzer was forced to resign because he was involved in a prostitution scandal. Spitzer was extremely bright and aggressive. I had admired and respected him when he served as Attorney General because he was very good at what he did. When he became Governor, I was hoping he'd succeed. In that role, he said he was a steamroller and was going to do things his way. I believed that was an indication he wasn't going to be successful and unfortunately it turned out he had problems.

David Paterson, who had been Spitzer's running mate, was asked to serve out the two years of his term. Paterson is the first African American to hold that position. I knew him for many years prior to him becoming Governor while he was going through college and law school. David is so knowledgeable and exceptional. He has a great sense of humor and is very gifted as a speaker who can make you smile at any presentation. He once told a funny story about running the marathon in New York City. Because he's sight-impaired, he was at the back of the line. He heard the gun go off and he said he felt like he was running for twenty minutes when he heard then Mayor Rudy Giuliani's voice. He said, "Where are we?" Giuliani said, "You just got to the starting line." Paterson really laughed about that. He was a good man and easy to work with. When he was first appointed Governor, I said, "David, how are you handling this?" He said, "Who asked for this?" He made me laugh.

Over the years I heard from quite a number of constituents who had been the victims of predatory towing of their vehicles in places where there were inadequate "no parking" signs. Lot owners were apparently receiving kickbacks from towing companies and consumers who were forced to locate their vehicles and pay exorbitant fees in cash to retrieve them. So I put a stop to it, passing legislation prohibiting lot owners from receiving a commission or share of the towing company's charges for towing and/or storing the vehicle. It also required that signs be posted in a conspicuous location, and must include the name and telephone number of the commercial tower and the address where the vehicle may be reclaimed.

I secured $125,000 for South Nassau Communities Hospital for the continued development of its newly opened Center for Cardiovascular

Health, which provides life-saving cardiac care available nowhere else on the South Shore of Nassau County. "On behalf of the South Nassau family, I thank Assemblyman Weisenberg for securing this generous grant and for his ardent support of South Nassau," said Joseph Quagliata, South Nassau President and CEO.

I also secured $125,000 to create a wall of names as part of the Nassau County Firefighters Museum and Education Center in Garden City, memorializing Long Island's bravest; our firefighters who died in the line of duty along with those who gave fifty or more years of service. "With Harvey Weisenberg's help, we will be celebrating the selflessness of Nassau County firefighters who lost their lives," said Frank Saracino, the Museum's Director of Grants.

I have worked hard to support summer programs for our local communities and for people with and without disabilities. With the help of Michael Alon of Cedarhurst and David Weingarten, whose son Adam, then twenty-seven, has Downs Syndrome, I was able to bring in a grant of over $250,000 to Nassau County. We wanted to create a playground where children with autism and other physical, sensory, developmental, or cognitive disabilities could play side-by-side with other nondisabled peers. The County worked with the nonprofit group "Let All the Children Play" to develop a two-acre universally accessible playground within Eisenhower Park in East Meadow. It was modeled after a playground in Israel and was the first of its kind in Nassau County.

"This initiative will drastically improve Nassau County's recreational accessibility and integration,"' said David Weingarten, Executive Director of Let All the Children Play. "We are grateful to have Assemblyman Weisenberg's support. His enthusiasm and devotion to children with special needs will allow this project to improve the lives and dignity of all children in Nassau County."

Also in 2008, I was able to obtain $100,000 in funding so that the Long Beach School District could offer—for the first time—a summer recreation program for students with disabilities. It ran in cooperation with the city's Recreation Department.

I secured another $125,000 for repairs and upgrades to the Bishop Molloy Recreation Center in Point Lookout. These included bathroom and kitchen renovations and a ceiling repair so that groups of all religious and ethnic backgrounds could hold meetings and events at this popular facility, which has served the community since 1947. I also wrote a check for $50,000 since I used to run recreation summer programs there, so I was familiar with the people and the building. There's a plaque in the community center thanking us.

I obtained another $125,000 for AHRC's Camp Loyaltown, the nonprofit summer residential respite camp I referred to earlier. The grant was to make hilly paths more accessible to those in wheelchairs and in need of ambulatory assistance.

I've been a lifeguard for sixty years, and have had many interesting, even unbelievable experiences. But one of the most unusual was an experience that was so unique that it was written up in *American Lifeguard* magazine. I had been patrolling the beach on Labor Day in 2008, and I saw something floundering in the water. I took a torp, which is rescue equipment, and headed out to investigate. The surf was rough that day, and the beach had been red flagged. But if someone or something needs saving, it's my job to help, and help was, in fact, needed. Not by a human though. By Henry, a falcon, believe it or not, who had been doing his job, chasing birds away from the runways at Kennedy Airport. He had gotten "fowled" up (pun intended) by some wires (put there by his owner to track him). I thought he was struggling to stay afloat in the rough surf.

I love animals, and was happy to do my job, just as Henry had been doing his. The falcon belonged to Erik Swanson of the Falcon Environmental Service. Erik was so appreciative. "It was pretty impressive," he told the magazine, "for Harvey to go into the water and rescue the falcon." Maybe so. I was just doing my job. I'm only grateful I didn't have to give it mouth-to-beak.

When I was reelected in 2006, I received seventy percent of the vote, a margin that was typical of my election victories. In 2008, I was opposed by Mike McGinty, who I have always liked, and who is the mayor of Island Park. I said at the time that "I admire him as a public servant, but this is the wrong place and the wrong time. This is going to be the most difficult time to serve in Albany. They need a strong voice to advocate on a bipartisan basis to have success."

What Mike had to say at the time was very interesting. "I am not running against Weisenberg," he said. "I am running against the Assembly. I think the voters think it's time for a change."

Well, the voters didn't see it that way. The final vote tally was 31,568 to 16,148 so I won my tenth term. I not only defeated my Republican challenger for State Assembly in my own City of Long Beach, I outpolled President Obama, my seventy-five percent to his sixty-one percent. I am proud of the service I have given to our communities, and am just as proud that the feeling is mutual.

I am also proud to be a supporter of education, learning, and literacy at every age. I was awarded the first, and I believe only, Library Champion Award from the Nassau County Library System for my support of local libraries, not only of their mission of literacy, but also of the importance of maintaining local, community control of our libraries. Immediately following the announcement, I received a nice letter from U.S. District Court Judge Arthur Spatt who wrote, "In my view, this award was well-earned by an outstanding elected official."

I believe in recognizing quality, hardworking public servants, whatever their party affiliation. I dedicated one of my 2008 newsletters to Jesse Mistero, a Republican leader from the Five Towns who had passed away. I remembered him as a kind and caring individual who was always willing to extend a helping hand, and who was always there for his community. That's what it's all about.

A unique project, of which I am very proud, is a book I published along with Eric and Hedy Page, who owned a local art and framing shop called Follow Your Art. Hedy, a world-renowned, talented artist, saw Ricky at an event, and asked to sketch him. She did, and the result was beautiful. She then suggested that she visit facilities and sketch what she saw, the people, both caregivers and those receiving care. The result was our book *The Beauty of Our Special Children, Putting a Face on Those With Disabilities and Those Who Care for Them*. She worked on the book for four years, and I paid for the publication, and dedicated the book to her special family member, Eric's mother Anna, who, along with much of their family, perished in the Holocaust.

I gave the book to many people, one of whom happened to be Governor David Paterson. He sent me a lovely note. "This wonderful book is an embodiment of your enduring commitment to children and adults with disabilities. Over the decades, your tireless efforts and passionate advocacy have empowered countless special needs individuals to lead productive and rewarding lives, reminding them and others of their irreplaceable contributions to society."

2009—Leandra's Law

Drunk driving is the scourge of our roads and highways, and drunk drivers not only must be punished, they should be stopped before they start driving. Following the death of a Suffolk County police officer after a crash involving an allegedly drunk driver, I introduced a bill that would make mandatory the use of ignition interlock devices, which measure blood alcohol via the breath, when a driver has been convicted of driving while intoxicated a second time within five years of the first infraction or at the discretion of a judge. I brought this bill twice, the second time following the Suffolk officer's death since, as I said in *Newsday*, "this tragedy was so preventable."

I agree with Deena Cohen, then president of the Long Island Chapter of Mothers Against Drunk Driving, who said, "there is absolutely no downside" to this device. And when children are the victims, driving while intoxicated is particularly despicable. At that time on average, five-hundred children were killed each year in alcohol-related traffic crashes, where the adult driver was responsible for their safety. So I introduced a bill increasing penalties across the board to any impaired driver who drives with, causes serious injury to, or causes the death of a child under sixteen.

Ultimately, my efforts resulted in Leandra's Law which, like so many pieces of worthwhile legislation, was the result of a tragedy. Drunk drivers with blood-alcohol contents of 0.08 or higher who have child passengers age fifteen or younger, now faced a possible prison sentence from sixteen months to four years imprisonment and fines of as much as $5,000. The law also strengthened the penalties for first-degree vehicular manslaughter, aggravated vehicular assault, and aggravated vehicular homicide. Additionally, a person charged with the new first-time felony would be limited in their ability to plea bargain. Arresting officers in these situations were now required to contact New York State Child Protective Services, where warranted, if the offending driver was the parent, guardian, or was otherwise legally responsible for a child passenger.

"This is the right decision, not just for my daughter, but to prevent something like this from happening again," said Lenny Rosado, father of eleven-year-old Leandra Rosado, who died when the intoxicated driver of a car carrying her and six other children flipped over on the Henry Hudson Parkway. This was the biggest bill of the year.

I dedicated one of my 2009 newsletters to "all of the families in New York State who have lost a loved one to a drunk driver. You will always be in my thoughts and prayers."

In February, we held public meetings about the controversial proposal to create an island for a Liquefied Natural Gas plant off the Long Beach shore, which had first come up in 2007. The importance of these sessions was to inform the public, so we could base whatever choices we made on real information, rather than hearsay. "Anything that would be negative to our beach," I said, "I would be adamantly opposed to. I'm not really thrilled with the idea, but as an educator, I feel that people should have access to information." The project did not come to fruition.

In April, Autism United and other advocacy groups held the first Autism Epidemic Day on the steps of the Capitol to lobby against proposed budget cuts to special education and early intervention services. So much had changed since I had first entered the Assembly in 1989. Then I felt like a lone voice advocating for special needs families. Now we had many voices speaking out on the issues that affected them. It was all about educating the people who were in a position to do something, as well as making them aware of what our priorities are. As I said about this rally, "The only thing we have in front of us is a desire to make people understand that people are more important than dollars."

I can recall a press conference with Governor Paterson, Secretary of State Lorraine Cortes-Vazquez, and Assemblyman David McDonough, a Republican, where we announced the appropriation of close to two million in state and federal funding that eased the burden on local property taxpayers. Nassau BOCES received one million to streamline several administrative functions which—listen to this—would save taxpayers a whopping $41.5 million over the next ten years. Six-hundred thousand went to Nassau County to consolidate waste water facilities in the villages of Lawrence and Cedarhurst. An additional quarter million was secured through the New York State Office of Children and Family Services for Nassau County's Department of Social Services, which was in dire need of additional Child Protective Services caseworkers.

I remember being photographed with, then, City Manager, the late Charles Theofan, as he thanked me for $300,000, which went to splash parks in the North Park neighborhood, the West End, and the East End Canal area.

That September, we had one-hundred and twenty special needs kids participate in the surfing program that had evolved since the first one in 2002. Surfer's Way, was a Long Beach based nonprofit I had founded with Long Beach local Eliot Zuckerman in 2002 when we went by the name of Surf Pals.

It was an honor to participate in the unveiling of the beautiful new Fallen Firefighters Memorial at the Nassau County Firefighters Museum and Education Center in Garden City. The memorial displays the names of Nassau County firefighters who have lost their lives in the line of duty. Among those names is that of fallen Malverne volunteer firefighter Paul Brady, who, you may remember, died tragically in 2006, and whose name was, for a time, denied inclusion on the New York State Fallen Firefighters Memorial Wall in Albany. I made it my personal mission to see that decision reversed and whether or not the Albany memorial included Firefighter Brady, which it did, I saw to it that a memorial was funded in Nassau County. In the center of our memorial wall, we have the names of firefighters from Nassau who perished on September 11, 2001. A kiosk tells the story of the lives and extraordinary deeds of those lost heroes, and there is a striking life-sized statue of a firefighter cradling a rescued child in his arms. The model for that statue was New York City firefighter Tom Gies, son of Merrick Firefighter Chief Ronnie Gies, who was killed on 9/11.

I have made it my business to always support our firefighters, and to do whatever I can to make that support tangible. I was an Honorary Chief of the Inwood and Atlantic Beach Fire Departments, Honorary Captain in the Oceanside Fire Department, and an honorary member of Woodmere and Meadowmere Park Fire Departments, as well as an Honorary Chief of the Second Battalion, which includes Baldwin, Freeport, Island Park, Long Beach, Oceanside, and the Point Lookout-Lido Department. Ellen and I frequently attended Firefighters Association of the State of New York (FASNY) regional legislative outreach meetings. So it was with particular pride that I accepted the 2009 Golden Trumpet Award from the FASNY. Tom Cuff, then FASNY President, noted that, "Harvey Weisenberg, in standing up for FASNY and the 130,000 volunteer firefighters and EMS personnel it represents on key issues and concerns, richly deserves this award." I was the only Long Island legislator to receive this award.

A controversial issue arose when I turned seventy-five. I had been in the New York State retirement system since 1952. I worked at all sorts of jobs that qualified, from shoveling coal at the Long Beach incinerator to being a police officer, a Councilman, and more. I had earned a pension, and I turned in my retirement papers in 2009 because, if I were to pass away without putting in for my retirement, my beloved Ellen would have received nothing, and we still had Ricky to worry about. So I put in for my retirement. This is perfectly legal. In fact, I could have done this ten years earlier. I also, again entirely legally, continued to earn a salary for being an active Assemblyman, which was about $79,500 a year then.

People wanted to know why I didn't make room for someone new. Why? God gave me a mission. I have a special child, and I was still able to do some good, for Ricky and for a lot of other people.

Some folks in the news came after me with a tenacity that surprised me. There was even an editorial cartoon about me in *Newsday*. But I had and have nothing to hide. I told them the truth. I earned my pension. I continued to earn my salary. It was all perfectly legal and all earned. I was defending a situation where there was no wrong-doing and was best for my family. They were upset, but I wasn't. It was their problem. Eventually those very same journalists came around.

2010—DWI Law Change

They say "all politics is local," but you know, sometimes it's international. In early 2010, I welcomed student intern Laura Murphy, a political science major at the University College in Cork, Ireland, to the State Assembly. I gave her a bouquet of flowers and a bright green Polar Bear garment, and Laura was able to further her studies by observing our state government in action.

At about the same time, I was able to have a $20,000 grant awarded to Long Beach Medical Center for their program to prevent underage drinking through better coordination with law enforcement, enhanced enforcement efforts, and reducing youth alcohol access. There was a photo in the newspaper of me thanking Karen Carpenter-Palumbo, Commissioner of the New York State Office of Alcoholism and Substance Abuse Services.

I helped to close what amounted to a loophole hindering the prosecution of drunken driving cases, when Governor Paterson signed into law a bill I sponsored. It allowed blood to be drawn on the say-so of a police officer by specially trained paramedics or EMTs at the scene of accidents involving drunken and impaired driving resulting in death and injuries. Until that time, a 1988 law required a physician's presence in order for blood to be drawn, which led to the suppression of important evidence in many DWI cases. "Today's signing is a giant step forward in ensuring justice," said Nassau District Attorney Kathleen Rice. "Joe McCormack, an assistant District Attorney in the Bronx, called the old law `an abomination.' I call it history."

I used to love swimming across our bay, but one day, I saw this orange water coming into the bay and I had no idea where it originated. Well, our Western Bay area is home to four sewage treatment plants and a power plant, which officials said discharged 64.5 million gallons of wastewater daily into the bay. Despite being hit with violations over the years, testing indicated that the levels of pollutants were still well beyond safe levels. So I was able to work with Dean Skelos to allocate $600,000 for research to find out what was in our bay, what was causing it, and where it was coming from. Our residents, swimmers, clammers, and boaters needed answers. The study was the culmination of seven years of work involving Nassau County and Long Beach City officials and environmental organizations, such as Operation SPLASH.

"We believe this study represents a new beginning for a cleaner, healthier Western Bays," said Adrienne Esposito, executive director of the Citizens Campaign for the Environment. The grant was awarded to scientists at Stony Brook University to find out what was polluting the water and what could be done about it. What we found was that a form of sea lettuce called ulva had built up, along with nitrogen from discharge from the local sewage treatment plants, combining to cause the stench.

I was also able to work with the Department of Environmental Conservation and the Town of Hempstead to obtain a permit. The project was to dredge nearly twenty-thousand cubic yards of sand to be added to Point Lookout beaches, while removing much of the offending seaweed. "Although we've known that there's pollution," I was quoted as saying in the newspapers at the time, "we've desperately needed this scientific evidence." And with that evidence in hand, I was able to take effective action.

When it was time for me to run again that year, many Democrats and Party officials were not happy about all of the bipartisan work I had been doing and the fact that I was friendly with Republicans at every level of government. But the fact was, those relationships benefited my constituents. I got results by working with whomever I had to work with. In the election that November, the voters supported the person who had been championing them for decades—I won an eleventh term.

Meanwhile, Paterson had decided not to run for a full term as Governor. Instead, Democrat Andrew Cuomo, the eldest son of Mario Cuomo, ran and won the election to become the fifty-sixth Governor of New York.

In December, I held a meeting for residents of Point Lookout at the Bishop Molloy Recreation Center, to address ongoing complaints by residents about noxious odors emanating from Reynolds Channel. The problem had apparently been going on for years, perhaps even a decade, but since a storm earlier that year had eroded quite a bit of the beach, large quantities of seaweed had washed ashore. The seaweed was thought by many to be the cause of the smell—identified as hydrogen sulfide—while some residents pointed accusing fingers at the Bay Park Sewage Plant, among other similar facilities. Residents complained of coughing, vomiting, and headaches, and said that when swiped across the outside of a window, one's finger came away with a dirty orange substance. I said that I believed the study of the pollution in the Western Bays would probably show a relationship between the growth of seaweed and the Bay Park Sewage Plant. I would be proven right.

2011—My Fifth Governor

The year opened with a new Governor, Andrew Cuomo. When I was in the presence of Mario Cuomo, I knew I was with a great person who cared about people. Matilda Cuomo is also a wonderful woman who worked in a group home for hearing impaired people for many years and was very much a supporter of the arts. She was a pleasure to be with. Having them come to Long Beach on occasions to be with my family, I felt close to the Cuomo family. So when Andrew Cuomo became the Governor, I offered my friendship and life experience to him. But he wasn't interested.

In fact, over time it became clear to me that in his position as Governor, he seemed to put himself above the most important people he had to work with, the Legislators. While we as State politicians tried to accomplish legislation to improve the quality of life and the ability to be able to survive in our state, in my previous experience with other Governors this would only occur when we worked together. Andrew Cuomo wanted to work by himself using the power of his office. He wanted to propose legislation that has to be passed by both houses. The Legislators legislate and the Executive approves, but it has to be passed by the Legislature and then the Governor has the ability to veto or sign. When it came to providing funding to the State budget to help the special needs community, I begged him to come to our house to see for himself what it is like to care for a person with special needs before he made decisions that would negatively affect us. He never did.

Regardless of my feelings about how Andrew Cuomo governed, I had to work with him for the needs of the people of the State of New York, and we did work together to pass meaningful legislation. I always felt because of my history with his family I wanted him to be successful in helping all the people of this state.

By February, we had the preliminary results of the SUNY Stony Brook study, which confirmed that the Western Bays were polluted. According to data from Stony Brook's School of Marine and Atmospheric Studies, the water in the bays between East Rockaway and Long Beach, which includes Reynolds Channel, had an abundance of nitrogen, which fuels the growth of seaweed. The nitrogen came from the treated effluent discharged from four treatment sewer plants in the area, which state and county officials said release 64.5 million gallons of wastewater into the bays daily. Further, they discovered contaminants found in cosmetics, fabric softener, and disinfectants. This was the most comprehensive study of the bays ever conducted. The two-year study was to be completed in 2012, with the goal to improve the water quality. As I said at the time, although we knew there was pollution, we desperately needed this scientific evidence so that the County can secure federal funding to commence cleanup.

I have always been a champion of open, accountable government. I have voted in favor of every piece of ethics-related legislation ever put before me. In early 2011, I stood with former New York Mayor Ed Koch and signed his New York Uprising pledge, which advocated for reform in budgeting, ethics, and redistricting.

Governor Andrew Cuomo sent me a post-session letter in which he wrote, "The historic ethics reforms of this Session will be a lasting legacy of our collective effort to restore integrity, performance, and public confidence back to New York State government." Thank you, Governor.

The year 2011 was also a year in which I forcefully advocated to limit tax increases, bringing relief to Nassau County and Long Beach businesses and families. Measures I supported capped the rate of tax increases in Nassau County, and limited Long Beach increases, which had the effect of more equitably distributing property tax liabilities between businesses and residences. "This is excellent news," said then City Manager Charles Theofan, "because it helps maintain the stability of the tax rates for the City of Long Beach residents."

I secured a $50,000 grant to help our Fourth Precinct use technology to fight crime. The grant came from the Edward Byrne Justice Assistance Grant program, named for an officer who had been senselessly murdered in the line of duty. The grant paid for three new devices: preliminary breathalyzer tests to reduce DWIs; digital hand-held meters, which measure the degree of tint on a vehicle's windows; and license plate scanners, which make it easier for police officers to identify and apprehend criminals. I applaud all the brave men and women of the Nassau County Police Department for their determination in bringing down crime in our communities.

I brought legislation that prohibited insurance companies from refusing to issue or renew an auto insurance policy for the sole reason that the motor vehicle to be insured is used by a volunteer firefighter to travel to calls. "Assemblyman Weisenberg has been a stalwart supporter of fire fighters," said Freeport firefighter Ray Maguire. "His loyalty and dedication . . . touch every firefighter in New York State."

I helped to make the waterways patrolled by the East Rockaway Fire Department much safer when I secured a $50,000 grant enabling the Department to purchase a much-needed, sufficiently equipped boat to provide both rescue and fire protection services in the bays, canals, and coastal areas.

Together with other local leaders, I took part in the dedication of the bridge that connects Long Beach with Island Park, which became known as the Michael Valente Memorial Long Beach Bridge. Michael

Valente was a longtime friend, a hero who volunteered, as a member of the 27th Infantry Division, to lead an attack on machine gun nests that had his unit pinned down. His bravery would lead to his being awarded the Medal of Honor, the highest distinction that can be earned by a member of our armed services. He received that honor from President Herbert Hoover in 1929. Michael was with us until the age of eighty. When I think of Michael Valente, I think of him as giving, loving family man, and as a model for us all. He loved his community and his country.

In June 2011, New York State legalized same-sex marriage, which was history-making. Some of my fellow Long Island lawmakers voted against the bill, and there were extensive debates in Albany and throughout society as to the merits of legalizing same-sex marriage. While some would call attention to what behavior they might perceive as moral or immoral, I must respectfully disagree. The issue is not about sex, it's about the Constitution of the United States of America. The issue is equality for all. We either have it or we don't. "It's discriminatory to deny people their rights, according to the Constitution," I was quoted as saying in *Newsday*. "I think anyone who wants to give love to each other and to the world, should be allowed to do so. I think people should accept people for who they are."

Within days of the change in the law, Ellen and I attended an enormous, beautiful wedding reception for hundreds of same-sex couples at the Carlyle on the Green in Bethpage State Park. It was a very happy day, and love was the big winner.

I dedicated my summer 2011 newsletter to Penny Ellis, The Best of the Best! Penny, who taught special education in Oceanside, was the winner of the 2011 Top Teacher Search sponsored by *Live! With Regis and Kelly.*

I sponsored a bill, along with Senator Carl Marcellino, a Republican from Syosset, which addressed what was then a new issue, texting while driving. For the first time, drivers could now be stopped solely for texting, playing games, or viewing photos while in motion, as opposed to being cited only after being pulled over for another offense. "The distraction of just one text message while driving can bring devastating and tragic consequences," I said at the time. Governor Cuomo signed my bill into law in July.

A "special and uplifting" event, as I called it then, that brought smiles to a lot of faces, including my own, involved Cliff and Will

Skudin and Jim Mulvaney. Their organization, *Surf for All*, held "Surfing for the Visually Disabled" and "Surfing for Diabetes" events that helped people with challenges to overcome fears, build self-esteem and confidence, and develop mutual support. *Surf for All* started in 2002 as a surf program for developmentally disabled teenagers. Over the years, the program has included children and adults with developmental delays, those on the autism spectrum, and many others. They provide surf lessons for students ages five to twenty during a summer special education program. They also work closely with Wounded Warriors, providing lessons and support for our military heroes and their families. As they say, while some of their students can't walk, speak, or see, once they're in the water on a surfboard, they experience a sense of independence and freedom that often cannot be demonstrated in other more traditional settings.

Cliff Skudin was very kind, saying, "Harvey Weisenberg has been a big supporter of *Surf for All*. He's an amazing individual." I could say the same for the whole Skudin family, whom I have known forever. "Look at the happiness we're giving these children and their families," I said at the time. "I love the good things we get accomplished. I'm involved because I love it." Who wouldn't love children with challenges who are developing courage and self-esteem through learning to surf? I am still involved with this program to this day.

I was pleased to announce that August the elimination of salt-water fishing license fees, which sent $300,000 worth of refunds to recreational fishermen and charter boat operators who bought recreational marine fishing licenses, as well as those who purchased lifetime fishing licenses.

Now and then, I get to see that I made a bit of a difference, often because of the thank yous that come my way. So I was proud and humbled to receive the New York State STOP-DWI Coordinators' Association's top honor, the Senator William T. Smith Award, at the Highway Safety Symposium. The award was particularly meaningful because it was given by the top District Attorneys in the state, which included at that time: Chris Cernik, the Association's Counsel; Jon Sullivan, Chairman; Maureen McCormick, Chief Vehicular Crimes Bureau, Nassau County District Attorney's Office; and Joe McCormack, Chief, Vehicular Crimes Bureau, Bronx County District Attorney's Office. I am the only one who ever received this award downstate.

A related thank you came my way from the AAA of New York at the Community Traffic Safety Awards Luncheon in East Meadow, where I received the Outstanding Achievement in Traffic Safety Award. The thank yous mean a lot, particularly because they represent lives saved.

I am all about protecting our vulnerable populations, and while that often means people with disabilities, it also means all children. At the time Megan's Law was enacted, unlawful surveillance was not really a serious offense and was treated like a peeping Tom situation. With the advance of recording equipment being more readily available and more easily hidden, this became a big problem with no felony level law to charge people with. So unlawful surveillance became a felony, but because Megan's Law was already written, that charge did not automatically put someone convicted of unlawful surveillance on the sex offender's list.

As a result, I was particularly proud to stand with Governor Andrew Cuomo when he signed into law legislation I had authored to correct this. It requires people convicted of "unlawful surveillance" to register as a sex offender. "Those who attempt to take inappropriate pictures or video of someone without that person's knowledge should be required to register as sex offenders, and that's what this new law does," I said in the press. "This law closes a loophole that has allowed too many sexual deviants to get a slap on the wrist for this heinous crime." I said then and I say it now: Information is the best defense against these predators.

But I wasn't done yet; I went even further, helping enact measures banning sexual predators from using social networking sites, creating the crime of child luring, and allowing citizens to sign up for email notifications about the presence of sex offenders in their communities.

Another vulnerable population I have defended is our pets. I was named the Honorary Chair of the American Kennel Club and International Cat Association's very popular Meet the Breed's event in November at the Javits Center in New York City. The event was the world's largest showcase of dogs and cats, and offered pet lovers a unique opportunity to play with some of the country's rarest dog and cat breeds, while educating themselves about responsible pet ownership and choosing the right pet for their lifestyle. I have long been a friend to our pets, despite their not being registered voters. "In my profession, it's a special pleasure to spend time with some truly nonpartisan creatures," I was quoted as saying at the time. "Dogs and cats ask so little of us, yet enrich our lives immeasurably. I am thrilled to have served as Honorary Chair."

I am also proud to have sponsored Buster's Law, which charges animal abusers with harsher penalties for causing extreme physical pain or acting in an especially cruel way towards animals. I also authored legislation to help brave and loyal service dogs who serve as guide dogs, hearing dogs, and detection dogs. It is my honor and a pleasure.

2012—Abuse of the Disabled

In February, I was able to announce that Governor Andrew Cuomo had signed into law a chapter amendment to my legislation, which requires the Office for People with Developmental Disabilities (OPWDD) to provide group homes and institutions with the criminal history of prospective employees. This ensured that OPWDD had the time needed to properly create the prior-abuse notification system required by my legislation. My legislation had unanimously passed both houses of the Legislature in 2011. It allowed OPWDD providers to request information from the agency on criminal history of job applicants and volunteers, in addition to any reports filed against them for abuse or neglect of an individual with developmental disabilities.

While I have been a legislator, a police officer, and of some help to people with special needs, I try to remember that as a teacher, I am committed to helping all children. Nowadays, with smartphones and Facebook and the advances we see every day in technology, we must remember the importance of a very critical skill, reading. So in early 2012, I was pleased to honor some children for exactly that. At the Peninsula Public Library in Lawrence, I helped to honor four-hundred and twenty-five children, age four to twelve, for reading more than four thousand books, more than any other Nassau County group of readers during the Monster Jam Winter Reading Program.

The Peninsula Library is a great place. "By consistently promoting literacy and education," I was quoted at the time, "the Peninsula Public Library proves again it is one of our top libraries in the County and one that plays an important role in our community." And that is still very much the case. I am a major supporter of literacy. I am proud to have been the only recipient of the Nassau County Library System and its fifty-four member libraries of the Library Champion award for my advocacy of local control of local public libraries.

In April, Long Beach—and Ellen and I—experienced the loss of a dear friend. Father Tom Donohoe was the Parish Priest at St. Mary of the Isle Roman Catholic Church in Long Beach for twenty-seven years. Born in West Hempstead, Father Tom went to seminary in Huntington, was ordained in 1962, and served in Bohemia, then at Nassau University Medical Center (back when it was called Meadowbrook Hospital). He was also an associate pastor at St. Elizabeth's Parish in Melville/Dix Hills for eight years.

On his first night in Long Beach in 1980, Father Tom Donohoe came to visit Ellen and me, and we spent over four hours making him aware of the diversity of the people of Long Beach and of the love that exists throughout our small city. Father Tom was a hands-on priest with every agency that dealt with helping people in our community, temple, or church. Father Tom served the people in Long Beach, Lido Beach, and Point Lookout since his arrival. "He touched so many people's hearts," said Sister Fran Monuszko, a Dominican sister who worked closely with him. He founded the Long Beach Interfaith Committee and was honored as the organization's Man of the Year in 2006. He was also chaplain for the Long Beach and Point Lookout-Lido Fire Departments, and the Long Beach Auxiliary Police. Father Tom retired from St. Mary's in 2007, but continued to serve at Our Lady of Miraculous Medal in Point Lookout, assisting with mass and services.

Father Tom was a part of our family. He visited our daughter Julie in Boston when he was on retreat, and they spent many hours together. He was close to and loved Ricky. When Father Tom's health was failing, the Bishop William Murphy wanted to send him out of town to recuperate, and doing what I do best—causing trouble—I spoke up, saying, "You can't send him away from his family, and Long Beach is his family." The Bishop won that one.

Father Tom Donohue died April 18, 2012. We all miss him at Artie's fish restaurant, where we used to have dinner on occasion. When I go there, I still look for him. Father Tom was truly loved by all.

I was on hand to celebrate the ninetieth birthday of Long Beach at a commemoration on June 3, 2012 at Kennedy Plaza. I remember feeling so grateful to have grown up here and to still be a part of this special city, while at the same time feeling that much has changed. I was also aware that some of the younger generations will find life more challenging because they don't have some of the positives my generation has enjoyed. "We're a microcosm of the United States, very diverse," *Newsday* quoted me as saying at the time. "The things I love most in this world don't cost money. The boardwalk, the sunset, the beach, being in the ocean. Everybody cares about everybody and that's what makes Long Beach great."

As I've said before, sometimes in between the very serious issues I championed, I was asked to consider some that were a little lighter, but of no less importance to the person bringing them to my attention. A woman I met at a convention put on by the American Kennel Club suggested I designate the German shepherd as the state dog. I like animals, so I agreed. The bill didn't go anywhere, as there was a competing bill at that time designating any rescued dog as the State dog. I think that was also a good idea. And while this sort of measure might not carry the weight of, say, lowered taxes, it may be more relevant perhaps than another measure up for a vote at that time; that black dirt be designated the State dirt. If you are a dirt supporter of any color dirt, please do not take offense.

The abuse of people with special needs who live in institutions, and who cannot speak up for themselves, finally became a reality when I passed Jonathan's Law in 2007. However, a provision under that law prohibited the sharing of that information with an outside party. The records would arrive stamped in big bold letters that read "confidential; do not disclose." Well, we put a stop to that, amending Jonathan's Law in 2012 to allow family members to share reports of abuse with health care providers, law enforcement, and the recipients' attorney. This clarification helped families seek justice for their loved ones who, through no fault of their own, have had to face abuse.

While this always mattered to me for everyone's children, it had become personal. I was on the mental health committee in the Assembly. We held hearings where it was brought to view that OPWDD, an agency established to protect our special needs population, had admitted that from 2008 through 2012 there were eighty-three thousand cases of neglect and abuse and less than five percent had been investigated. The law that Governor Cuomo was considering signing in October would establish the Justice Center for the Protection of People with

Special Needs to investigate claims of abuse and neglect and create a statewide registry of workers in public and private facilities who have committed acts of abuse and prevent them from working with people with disabilities. I'll add more on that in the 2013 section.

Many victories are long fought and hard won. Some take years of fighting to win. And so it was with recognizing the line of duty deaths of two Long Island volunteer fighters. Paul Brady, of the Malverne Fire Department and Wilbur Ritter, of the Sayville Fire Department both died within a month of each other in July and August of 2006, respectively. Both deaths were clearly line of duty deaths, as each man was performing the duties of a firefighter at the time of their deaths. I referenced this earlier in this chapter.

Unfortunately, at that time, problems were brewing in Albany among the members of the New York State Fallen Firefighters Memorial Committee, which is charged with formalizing the names to be included on the tribute Memorial Wall in Albany each year. The wall includes the names of all firefighters killed in the line of duty. When it was created, the memorial committee was comprised of representatives of both paid and non-paid firefighters, with the paid firefighters having a majority. I'm sure the creators of this meaningful memorial never foresaw the acrimonious struggles that would unfold in 2006. To my utter shock, the committee denied the inclusion of Paul Brady's and Wilbur Ritter's names on the wall. In the absence of any real explanation, it seemed the volunteer firefighters had come to the conclusion that the deaths of paid firefighters should not be mourned as equally as the volunteers; another example of bad actors in positions of power.

On Long Island, Paul and Wilbur's colleagues were deeply distressed, and their families dealt an unspeakable insult during their time of grief. I began a mission to ensure they would be given the recognition and esteem they deserved for making the ultimate sacrifice in volunteer service to others. It took six years of negotiating with feuding factions, a few unsuccessful non-legislative approaches and asking for the intervention of four different governors during turbulent times (Pataki, Spitzer, Paterson, and Cuomo). Finally, in 2012, I was able to secure unanimous passage of a bill in both houses that forced the memorial committee to recognize not only Paul Brady and Wilbur Ritter, but all line of duty deaths in the future. The bill was signed by Governor Cuomo in July 2012.

Three months later, Paul and Wilbur were added to the wall during the annual ceremony in Albany. Along with thirteen family members, we tearfully celebrated our shared success. "I'm absolutely thrilled," said Paul's widow, Lisa Brady. "Paul deserves to be honored." And with his name in its proper place on the Albany monument, after six years of fighting, Paul and Wilbur will now be forever honored.

In appreciation of this longtime-coming victory, I was made an honorary chief of the Malverne Fire Department.

Government is a strange beast, more often than not, and at times is just unbelievable. Where else could a bill sponsored by the Senate Majority leader not be brought for a vote by its own sponsor? But that's just what happened when State Senator Dean Skelos sponsored a bill designed to help relieve Long Beach of its then $10 million deficit. This was a vital piece of legislation for our city, which had been struggling under the weight of debt at the time, as the new City Manager took office. But Senator Skelos walked away from his own bill. Why? Politics. County Executive Ed Mangano was unhappy with Skelos over another issue, and there was a perception that the Assembly refused to help Nassau County, so turnabout being fair play, the Senate lost interest in helping Long Beach.

After the fact, Senator Skelos was quoted in *Newsday* as saying that he had only introduced this borrowing bill for Long Beach, "as a courtesy." Skelos and Republicans in the State Senate did not believe that borrowing was a "wise way" to get out of debt, said Scott Reif, a spokesman for Skelos. "Our position is you get your fiscal house in order through reducing spending," Reif said.

All of this took place just after the Long Beach City Council had passed a budget that included a 7.9 percent tax hike; contingent on deficit financing that would pay down the deficit over ten years. As a result of being turned down by the Senate, our city now had to consider a much steeper tax increase. "These guys didn't cause the financial mess that exists; they inherited it," I said at the time.

An ongoing problem that is occurring right now is the danger posed to pedestrians, bicyclists, and skateboarders, especially children and teens, by motor vehicles that are driving too fast on our local roadways. After an eighth grade boy was struck and seriously injured, I introduced a bill that enabled Long Beach and Town of Hempstead officials to reduce speed limits on many local roads. Mary Beth Thurston, a school nurse at Long Beach Middle School, witnessed two such accidents. "Two middle school students have been hit by cars in the last two weeks in the same stretch of road," Thurston said. "There are four schools within a half mile of this stretch. Our lawmakers should help make it safer." And that's exactly what we did.

The roadways are not our only dangerous thoroughfares. Think about this: How do you know what pollutants are in our local waters? Well, in June I helped pass the Sewage Pollution Right to Know Act, which now provides immediate public notice when discharges of untreated or partially treated sewage entered the waterways. "Families need to know that the water they are swimming or fishing in is not going to pose a health risk," I said at that time. This immediately impacted Reynolds Channel by providing monitoring of the Bay Park Sewage Treatment Plant in East Rockaway.

I love the beach, but the incidence of melanoma has been rising steadily. So I sponsored a bill that made tanning salons off limits for anyone sixteen years of age or younger. "The harmful effects of ultraviolet exposure accumulate over time," I explained, "which means skin damage inflicted at an early age can cause major health problems down the road." The vice president of advocacy for the northeast of the American Cancer Society called this a "significant protection," for these young people. Originally, we had proposed the ban for seventeen-year-olds as well, but after the tanning industry raised objections, we lowered the age limit to sixteen in order to pass the Senate.

Up until then, 2012 was a good year for me, and by extension, for the people of my district. The New York Public Interest Research Group published an analysis that documented that among all Long Island Assembly members, I had the second highest number of bills signed into law. Democrat Bob Sweeney of Lindenhurst, a committee chair, had the most. Bob Sweeney often had opportunities for leadership in some of the highest levels of the Assembly, but his dedication and love of the environment was his professional priority. Not many people would turn down a pay raise to follow what he thought was most important to him in his career. When Sweeney is not working in the Assembly, he volunteers to work with people with disabilities in other countries. He's also a great fisherman. He goes to Alaska to "catch the big one."

That summer, I was honored to be named "Legislator of the Year," by the New York State Association of Chiefs of Police.

And then on October 29, Hurricane Sandy hit New York. What does one say about a natural disaster that adversely affected our entire community? Most of Long Beach was underwater, homes and businesses were lost, cars ruined, but the spirit of our residents, though battered, persevered.

The night of the storm, during high tide and beneath a full moon, Ellen and I watched awestruck as the angry ocean rushed in, then up, and under our seventeen-foot-high boardwalk, ripping it apart, and sending it all over town. That dark night, I remembered hearing about another storm of similar magnitude, seventy-eight years before when I was just a small boy. But this night, with this furious storm, which came after decades of social and business growth and prosperity, we had much more to lose.

We watched as cars were washed away. Four-hundred thousand cars were lost in Sandy. Sand cascaded into our streets, which were lined with debris, and would soon be teeming and piled high with the soggy possessions of our residents, whose courage and resilience have been an inspiration. Our local workers and officials worked tirelessly, for days, weeks, and months on end fighting to restore our lives and services.

Ellen and I were determined to stay with our community during this time of need. We lived for weeks without electricity, heat, or water. For a while I had to haul up buckets of water from outside to flush the toilets. We traveled to the North Park area and made sure the hole in the roof of the MLK Center was repaired and worked with MLK's director, James Hodge, to make sure the facility would be able to serve the residents of that neighborhood. Food and supplies were distributed from the Center, and school buses from closed and damaged schools continued to bring children, who were given hot meals. The facility was short on food and needed funding, so Ellen and I donated $10,000 for food supplies for residents.

My Long Beach office was flooded and closed. I know people were seeking help there. I had my non-working office phones forwarded to my Albany office, where we triaged hundreds of callers round-the-clock who were in immediate need of assistance with basic safety and shelter during lengthy utility outages. We located elderly and other vulnerable people who had lost touch with their nonresident families and handled disputes and information on insurance policies and claims procedures, emergency health situations, and banking disputes involving damaged property equity. This was all before FEMA was situated and long before New York Rising was established.

In November I was seventy-eight and we had another election, in the middle of our Superstorm Sandy recovery. I ran for re-election again and won a twelfth term. But there was no time for celebration as the long road to recovery of District 20 was ongoing.

2013—$90 Million Restored

After months of utter devastation, as we climbed back into some semblance of normalcy, if you could call it that, I returned to Albany in January 2013 to do whatever I could to help secure state recovery resources and consider new laws and regulations that reflect what we learned as survivors of this catastrophe.

I sponsored the "Superstorm Sandy Assessment Relief Act," which applied to municipalities outside of New York City in counties declared a Sandy disaster area by FEMA. The bill authorized municipalities to lower the 2012-2013 tax assessments of properties that lost a particular percentage of their structural value due to the storm.

I sponsored a bill with Republican Senator Jack Martins that allowed the Long Island Industrial Development Agencies (IDAs) to assist retail businesses, which had been exempted from being eligible for aid until that point. The IDAs provided more than $3.4 million in sales tax exemptions to help lower recovery costs, and helped nearly two-hundred local businesses.

On January 5, we had a ceremony marking the demolition of the historic Long Beach boardwalk. It was a bittersweet day for me. I had been running on the boardwalk for sixty-five years; had gathered coins with my friends beneath it; and had worked summer jobs there as a teenager. The local newspapers ran a little piece in which I talked about my memories of our boardwalk. "The beautiful boardwalk and beach has been utilized to meet the needs of all people. It was a respite from the stresses of life. People came to the boardwalk to enjoy the tranquility, to socialize, to utilize the beauty of our beach to just sit and reflect. When I was a kid, there used to be people who used to come up here and sing to the ocean, and I remember, as a child, the Nassau Hotel was a five-star hotel, and we had people dress formally in suits. It was like a fashion show."

Of course, now we have a "smarter, stronger, safer" $44.2 million boardwalk. And it is terrific. So many of our officials did a great job in bringing us back: Senator Chuck Schumer, Dean Skelos, Ed Mangano, our Long Beach City administration, and of course, Governor Cuomo.

It took a while. Government, like God, moves slowly. But by April the federal disaster funding requested by Governor Cuomo had been approved and two connected programs were created: the New York Rising, which has helped so many of our homeowners rebuild and, in many cases, lift their homes, and the Community Reconstruction Program, which established local committees charged with identifying projects that require funds to complete recovery and reconstruction.

People from all over the country came to volunteer—police, fire departments, military personnel who gave out food, water, and other necessities—and gave of themselves to help our residents. Long Beach residents were left with so little, but whatever they had, they shared with each other and with those who came to our aid.

A true hero was Senator Chuck Schumer. When every aspect of our city was at its most desperate, he brought in an enormous generator from Caterpillar, which functioned essentially as CPR for some of our infrastructure and many of our residences. Senator Schumer was quite literally a lifesaver, because he brought us back from the abyss to the ranks of the living, in terms of the necessities of life. He made himself constantly available to me, as a State Legislator and a personal friend.

I sponsored a bill that would authorize the City of Long Beach to issue bonds up to $12 million to help with the post Superstorm Sandy recovery. We had tried to pass a borrowing bill the previous year, but politics got in the way. This time was different. The Senate vote was 56-0 to allow the bonds to be issued, and to be paid over ten years. The crux of the matter, as the *Herald* quoted me as saying, was this: "Allowing the city to issue bonds would shift much of the burden off local taxpayers! That's what it's all about."

Sandy had impacted the Bay Park Wastewater Treatment Plant that had been the subject of ongoing studies I mentioned previously. The odor that had led to the study only got worse after the storm. Along with then Nassau County Executive Ed Mangano and others, I urged the State and Federal government to expedite the release of funds in order to repair the troubled facility. We asked for $1.2 billion.

But soon I had another battle to engage in. In March, the Legislators passed its third on-time budget in a row. Buried in that fiscal plan was a $90 million cut in programs for the disabled. I would have none of that. *The New York Times* said: "The 2013 state budget contained a harsh $90 million cut to programs that serve children and adults with developmental disabilities. As a long-time advocate for those who rely on the impacted programs through the New York State Office for People with Developmental Disabilities (OPWDD), Assemblyman Weisenberg introduced legislation to restore the funding." But I wound up doing much more than that.

During an era when public servants are routinely called on the carpet and worse, I am proud to have been singled out by former Assemblyman and chair of the Ways and Means Committee, *Long Beach Herald* columnist Jerry Kremer. He pointed out that I was able "to get hundreds of thousands of dollars allocated to the needs of a wide range of disabled people." He wrote an article in June 2013 entitled "One Man Can Move Legislative Mountains," in which he eloquently painted a picture from the vantage point of one who has been there. In discussing the proposed $90 million funding cut, Jerry wrote: "If ever a document is written in stone, the state budget is it. . . . Once the spending plan is passed, it is the law for one year; with no changes." He wrote that, "There was no meanness behind the cut; the state had simply lost federal funds for those programs, and in turn the budget technicians cut the state funds."

The situation and the part I am gratified to have played in it were utterly unique. Money that is to be cut from the state's agreed-upon budget just isn't restored. It almost never happens. Jerry wrote that I "went toe to toe with a very powerful governor and won his battle, which is unheard of in Albany. . . .. The winners are the thousands of disabled people who are being cared for by hundreds of nonprofit agencies all over the state. . . .. 'It is better to light a candle than curse the darkness,' he wrote, quoting a Chinese proverb. "Harvey Weisenberg has done nothing less than start a bonfire." Amen.

Just prior to what would be an historic vote about the reinstatement of these funds, I was chatting with a writer for the magazine *City and State* about a discussion that had taken place in the Governor's office, with his budget director, his secretary, the Governor, and me just prior to the vote over the $90 million. What I said in that conversation was that "they're panicking. I have every member of the Assembly on my bill and the Senate promised to restore the money." This was printed in the newspaper, and the Governor was furious. I gave no press conference, I told him. This was a private conversation that was printed without my permission. Somehow I don't think that calmed him down.

In their article, *The New York Times* went on, "During the passage of the budget, the Assemblyman made a heartfelt plea to his colleagues and the public about the impact the cuts would have on the families and individuals served under the program. By the date of its passage in the Assembly, every member of the Assembly had joined Weisenberg in sponsoring the measure in that house and the issue had gained national attention."

Originally, $120 million in cuts had been proposed, but $30 million had been restored. A budget amendment had been proposed to restore the remaining $90 million, but had been defeated. Even though the bill had been turned down, and the barn door, so to speak, was already closed, I took to the floor, determined to have my say. If they were going to take the funding away, they'd have to hear a thing or two first! I talked about Ricky. I talked about Ellen. I talked about love and the meaning of public service. I questioned the priorities of our Legislators, aiming much of my speech at the Governor. "Have you ever fed a person who cannot feed himself?" I asked the speechless Assembly. "Have you ever changed an adult's diaper?" I demanded to know. "Who cares? Are our priorities upside down?" (If anyone wants to see this speech it's available on YouTube, Harvey Weisenberg on OPWDD Cuts, March 28, 2013.)

And every person there, both sides of the aisle, stood up and applauded. They were not so much applauding me as they were applauding their own values, which were, in effect, being restored to sanity. I was quoted by *The New York Times* as saying, "This much bipartisan support for anything is a rare commodity and speaks to the urgency of the situation."

I was honored by the agencies dubbing me "the voice of those who have no voice," and I addressed every member: "When you vote, you will be that voice of those who have no voice!" Now that's a responsibility, and the Assembly as one voice responded. In an unheard-of turn of events, the $90 million was restored.

The magazine *City and State* has a section called "Winners and Losers" in which readers, who are primarily elected officials, are polled as to who has had the most positive influence in a given period. In the June 17 issue, I was the leader in that poll, though I would agree with Jerry Kremer that the biggest winners were those people who would receive services that would otherwise have been cut. The publication wrote as part of that piece, "Your Choice— Harvey Weisenberg: The legislature's unofficial gym coach helped get $90 million in funding for disabilities services restored after being cut from the budget. His indefatigable advocacy convinced lawmakers to back the bill unanimously, after the governor huffed and puffed on the issue, but could not blow the people's house down."

On June 30, the Protection of People with Special Needs Act went into effect. It made changes to the requirements for the standards for the protection of day and residential students who attend a residential school (for example, the New York State School for the Blind, the New York State School for the Deaf, a State-supported school that has a residential component, a special education school district, or an approved private residential school).

It also established the Justice Center for the Protection of People with Special Needs, (mentioned earlier), which assumed the functions and responsibilities of the former Commission on Quality of Care and Advocacy for Persons with Disabilities. This new organization would ostensibly monitor people who receive care from six state agencies or licensed nonprofits. It would have a special prosecutor, inspector general, and hotline to report abuse, and would track abuses via a comprehensive database. The State's current record of investigating abuses in these facilities was dismal and, as we learned from Jonathan Carey, sometimes deadly. The Governor thought the new agency would fix the problem in institutions.

Now that sounds great, until you consider that this is really just a state agency investigating abuses within a state agency. Since the Justice Center was created, the statistics of abuse have not improved. More recently, convictions prosecuted by the Justice Center have been overturned by the courts because defendants have a right to be prosecuted by elected, not appointed, prosecutors. At least two predators of vulnerable people have been set free. It is unknown whether these two people are still working in the field. Our District Attorneys in New York State need to take definitive action to rectify this horrific situation. They need to learn how to prosecute these cases themselves and undo the concurrent jurisdiction they ceded to the Justice Center in the first place. I feel that the agencies that are supposed to achieve success in handling the system like the Justice Center or the OPWDD, as well as the justice system, fail to achieve any success in supporting the people they're supposed to protect.

The Associated Press reported on my amendment to Jonathan's Law in late 2013 that New York would no longer prohibit families from making use of once-secret reports that detailed abuse of their disabled relatives in state facilities. Jonathan's Law required the sharing of reports of abuse and neglect with families and guardians. Governor Cuomo signed the bill changing into law the amendment to Jonathan's law that halted this practice.

In August, I received "A Lifetime of Service and Achievement" award at the Silberman School of Social Work of CUNY Hunter College. The event was sponsored by New York City's Sinergia organization. "We are honored to host this special event that recognizes Harvey's exceptional accomplishments and service to the people of New York State over the past 50 years," said Myrta Cuadra-Lash, Sinergia Executive Director. "We thank the member agencies of the NYAEMP (the New York Association of Emerging and Multicultural Providers) and Sinergia for making this event possible and for acknowledging and appreciating the dedicated service of Assemblyman Harvey Weisenberg." "A thank you like this is very meaningful," I was quoted as saying at the time; very much so.

We live in a time when service to those who need it most seems to hold little value to those in control of budgets. It is a time of draconian cuts to services. The Harriet Eisman Community School, a division of Long Beach Reach, a valuable service provider here in Long Beach, was in desperate need of funding in 2013. The school graduated its first class in 1975, and since that time, has positively impacted the lives of more than sixteen-hundred young people who had been disenfranchised from mainstream academia.

"I knew that we could not lose the Harriet Eisman Community School and its programs, which are so important to individuals and families in our community," I said in a statement at that time. "This program has literally saved young people's lives." And it continues to do so to this day. I did what had to be done, and secured the $100,000 funding for this valuable institution to continue its good work.

In October, a little over a year since Hurricane Sandy, the Long Beach boardwalk was completed. We had a ceremony to mark the occasion on October 26.

2014—Time to Retire From the Assembly

In February, I was joined by one-hundred and two of my colleagues in a bipartisan effort to include a wage enhancement for direct caregivers in the 2014-2015 State Budget. The final budget included a two percent salary increase effective January 1, 2015. The message I gave then on the floor—and continue to talk about today—is that direct caregivers of our special people have one of the hardest jobs in the world, requiring the most responsibility, and most of them perform their duties with genuine love and care for those they serve. They are dedicated, hardworking, and very underpaid. So I was pleased to sponsor a cost-of-living pay increase for about one-hundred thousand caretakers of people with special needs for the 2015 year, followed by another the following year.

These were the first pay raises these vital caregivers had received in four years, which amounted to a real-world pay cut of eight percent. "Direct caregivers are entrusted with the well-being of some of New York's most vulnerable people," I said. "Their duties are often daunting, heartbreaking, and physically challenging." I have continued this fight even this year.

In May, I announced that I would not be seeking reelection. Ellen had dislocated her hip, and Ricky still needed our care. "It's time," I was quoted as saying in the *Long Beach Herald*. "Now I can just be with the person I love the most in the world, my wife, Ellen, and my children. I've accomplished most of everything that I want, but I still have things I want to fight for."

I had been blessed to have my wife with me in every aspect of my life. Serving in Albany for twenty-five years, I felt at the age of eighty, that it was now time for me to focus on what I love most, and that's being alone with my wife and with my family, and especially to be able to give more time and care to our special child, Ricky. While I retired as an elected official, I had not retired from pursuing my mission, to advocate for all people, especially those with developmental disabilities.

I was succeeded in the Assembly by another lifelong Long Beach resident, Democrat Todd Kaminsky, who was elected to the New York

State Assembly in November 2014. Because Long Beach continues to be a small city, Kaminsky is someone I have known since he was a kid. He used to lifeguard for me, and I know his family, who are very involved in the local community. He was a successful Federal prosecutor, so I was happy to support him when he took my seat. In 2015, he was named one of *City & State*'s 40 Under 40 Rising Stars. But following the expulsion of Dean Skelos from the State Senate, the Democratic Party selected him as their nominee for his seat in the special election in April 2016. He won that election and remains in that role today.

My life experience gives me the opportunity to use my influence and resources to be successful in achieving goals that I have set forth. I am proud to have spent much of my career reaching across party lines for causes for which we are united. Jim Moriarty, former Long Beach Republican Committee chairman and former City Councilman said upon my announced retirement, "Doing the right thing for Long Beach has always been first and foremost in his [my] mind. . ... Everybody knows Harvey and Ellen, and only has good things to say. . .."

Mike Zapson, former Long Beach Democratic Chairman, said, "Harvey has done a great job serving the community for a very, very long time, and he will be missed."

Morris Kramer, an environmentalist from Atlantic Beach, said, "He's been the single biggest force in protecting the barrier island's water supply."

In one of his columns, former Senator Al D'Amato wrote, "There are Democrats who work very hard to make sure that Long Island gets its fair share. We should pay tribute to one such leader, Assemblyman Harvey Weisenberg, a Long Beach icon who recently announced that he would be retiring after 25 years in the State Assembly. Over the course of his tenure, Weisenberg helped to pass more than 300 bills. He was always a tireless advocate for families who have children with special needs. Weisenberg always put his heart and soul into Long Beach and his South Shore district, and he will be sorely missed." Thank you, Al.

My retirement was a catalyst of sorts for several moving tributes. I was honored along with Ellen by South Nassau Communities Hospital at their 2014 Annual Carnation Ball in November, a wonderful event. The pool and workout facilities at the Long Beach Recreation Center were renamed the Harvey Weisenberg Aquatic and Fitness Center, which was a homecoming of sorts, honoring those many years before that I had been a swim instructor and the Recreation Supervisor, as well as a lifeguard.

In June, *Newsday* wrote a piece about me that was very emotional. "NY Assembly thanks Harvey Weisenberg for 25 years of helping people," read the headline. The article included the following: "I would like to rise and congratulate Harvey Weisenberg on one of the most successful tenures in the New York State Assembly we have ever seen," said Assemblyman Joseph Lentol, a Democrat from Brooklyn. "I don't think there is a larger persona who has helped the developmentally disabled in New York State. They are going to sorely miss you . . . those kids and those adults who have no voice except for you . . . You have done us proud."

To hear that from a colleague is very moving, and to hear similar words from Republicans perhaps even more so. "You leave a great legacy," said Republican Assemblyman Edward P. Ra from Franklin Square. "Thank you, on behalf of our county, Long Island and all of New York State." Republican Assemblyman Steven F. McLaughlin of Schaghticoke called me a "friend and mentor," while Assembly Majority Leader Joseph Morelle, a Democrat from Rochester, thanked me for my "extraordinary service to the state of New York."

I was asked to judge New York politics over twenty-five years. "It's diminished greatly," I said. "It appears that politics has taken over government, and dollars are more important than people. And it's upsetting." I viewed my work in the Assembly as public service. When politics takes over government, there is no government. Nevertheless, I'm really impressed with the new people who are coming in to serve in the Legislature, and I see under the strong leadership of the Speaker and Senate Majority Leader that we'll maintain dignity and respect from our legislators.

However, I still had work to do before I retired. Sometimes the families of young people with special needs are either not aware of services that are available to them or may not have access to those services. So I sponsored and passed a bill that required greater notification to parents and others who might be responsible for the student about their right to refer a student to the school district's Committee on Special Education (CSE) if a disability or mental health issue is suspected. We all recognize the parent, grandparent, or guardian's right to advocate for the young person in his or her charge. But the laws are not always apparent or transparent to the very people they were designed to help. This law, and with it the proactive provision of information about available services, removed some barriers to connecting the families with services.

Many services for people with special needs are aimed at people under the age of twenty-one, after which they "age out" of the system and must find other programs, geared to adults. The New York State Office for People With Developmental Disabilities has a program called The Front Door, which connects these adults with appropriate services. But as of 2014 there were approximately twelve thousand people on a waiting list for these adult services with four thousand of those considered critical needs.

So I wrote a bill, which required a plan to ensure critical needs are met in a timely manner, expedited the appeals process, provided assistance for persons seeking services, clarification of the process, and accelerated services for families in crisis. The bill was vetoed. Yet it appears that this is a problem that is only growing.

Meanwhile, there's a national issue when it comes to people with mental health problems and violent behavior. Government is not providing resources, and families cannot handle the obligation and responsibility with people who are a potential danger to themselves and others in our society. These issues aren't being adequately addressed and yet common-sense legislation is available if government wants to fix it.

As I do every year, I made a point of attending the 2014 Kristallnacht commemoration of the Holocaust Memorial Committee of Long Island, which I helped to establish, along with Dr. Robbins and Pearl Weill. Ellen and I were also proud to personally pay for the restoration of our city's Holocaust Memorial in front of City Hall.

Later that year, Long Beach Regional Catholic School honored me with their Community Service Award at their Crystal Ball, which was presented to me by Roni Danca, who had just retired as Long Beach Regional Catholic School's principal.

When he visited Albany in 2014, Cardinal Timothy Dolan conveyed kind words of encouragement, appreciation, and support for my longtime advocacy for people with disabilities and others who desperately need a champion in state government. His words brought tears to my eyes, but I smiled and responded that this was probably as close as I would ever get to meeting God.

I was also honored with the Young Israel of Long Beach's Community Service Award in July, presented by Young Israel's Rabbi Chaim Wakslak.

The Peninsula Counseling Center presented me with their 2014 Humanitarian Award, citing the millions of dollars in state funds I garnered for institutions at the heart of the communities in my district, schools, hospitals, libraries, police departments, fire departments, community, and recreation centers, as well as programs that serve children, the elderly, and those with disabilities.

These honors I received upon my retirement are all very special and I cannot single any out as more important than any other. I do, however, take special pride in being named the 2014 Advocate of the Year by the American Heart Association, because of the many lives saved by defibrillators I, with the help of the Acompora family, mandated throughout our state.

As I've said repeatedly, the rewards of my job are these wonderful thank yous that Ellen and I have been blessed to receive from the individuals, families, and institutions we have helped. But I am also proud to say that by the time I had retired from the Assembly, I had gotten three-hundred and thirty-seven bills signed into law. I went to Albany in 1999 hoping that I could make a difference beyond Long Beach for the people and causes I cared about. Twenty-five years later, while I understood there would always be more work to do, I was happy with what I had been able to accomplish.

8.

Ellen and Me in "Retirement"

One mid-June afternoon early in my time in the State Assembly, Ellen was with me on the floor of the New York State Assembly. She was the only spouse who regularly graced the Assembly floor. She noticed roses and carnations on all the Assembly members' desks, and asked why they were there. I played innocent and said, "Maybe somebody passed away." Then I pushed the button to address the house. What the New York State Assembly, and every office in the building heard was, "A flower is a symbol of delicate beauty and of love, and today we celebrate Ellen's birthday." Of course, Ellen blushed. Everyone applauded and sang *Happy Birthday* to her.

From that year on, I put flowers on the desks of every member of the New York State Assembly on June 15, so that we would remember to focus on this being a family day for everyone in the Assembly. It was a reminder that this job should not take over their lives, and members should appreciate the love of their families and of people, and not politics. Thank God for what you have. The Assembly, which I had been blessed to serve in for twenty-five years, is a family that is here to represent all of the people of the State of New York. It's about people, not politics.

That's why there was another annual June tradition I created nearly thirty years ago was to honor the Legislative Messenger Service who help keep the Senate and Assembly running smoothly every day. They deliver all the mail and documents around the Empire State Plaza and neighboring state buildings for Senate and Assembly legislators and their staffs. The messengers are all special people. Some are severely disabled; some are in wheelchairs. The program has been in place since 1973. I always honored them and told them they were the most efficient agency in the state of the New York and they only bring happiness to us. We started out with a pizza party and that evolved into big lunches and dinners. They loved Ellen. I did a resolution honoring them. The luncheons have continued since I retired thanks to Assemblyman Michael Benedetto, a Democrat from the Bronx. These workers were all part of our Assembly family.

But when I officially left the Assembly in June 2014, it was my family at home, specifically Ellen and also Ricky, that drew my attention. My life from the moment I met her was also about Ellen. We went everywhere together. She is in most of the photos of my time in the Assembly because she was with me for every event and recognition. She was a constant presence at my side, but also an active member of the community. She also had plenty of her own recognitions because she was also a warrior for causes that mattered to her, including those of special needs children and their families, and also, because of her own medical condition, the Juvenile Diabetes Research Foundation. She and I often wore matching outfits, like matching T-shirts or sweatshirts. When anyone commented, I saw it was a compliment.

Ellen and I really were one person; we were perceived that way. Our love for each other was admired by all, and we were often told how lucky we are for what we have. I thank God for the love and happiness Ellen and I have shared these past fifty years.

Even though I had retired from the Assembly I kept getting calls—and as I said in my introduction, I still do—from families seeking information on how to help their developmentally disabled family member. That's why in November 2015, Ellen and I founded the Harvey & Ellen Weisenberg Special Needs Resource Corp., to establish the Weisenberg Foundation. This is an advocacy organization that advocates for people who have no voice. Currently the Weisenberg Foundation is advocating for a raise in the wages of the direct caregivers who care for people with special needs, many of whom must work two, even three jobs to pay their bills.

The foundation Ellen and I created received the support and backing of the Alliance of Long Island Agencies, which is comprised of thirty-one member agencies that provide services to people with developmental disabilities in Nassau and Suffolk counties. The Alliance offers many services to its members, including advocacy and networking between members.

We also launched an online resource center for the families of caregivers and those with special needs, harveyandellenweisenberg.com. Our experience navigating through various agencies and programs to find the best care for Ricky was of course our inspiration. The website has a free smartphone app that provides users with information about social services programs and agencies catering to special needs residents. The app also provides access to laws aimed at protecting the developmentally disabled. It features video interviews with special needs families. To develop a virtual resource, we collaborated with a friend, Dave Feldman, who has a developmentally disabled niece. We had met a few years before during the making of a short film, *Everyone Deserves a Decent Life,* which won the Allen Fortunoff Humanitarian Film Award at the Long Island International Film Expo in 2014.

But though Ellen and I continued to battle for our child and for others, we had a more personal battle to confront. My beautiful Ellen, who had spent her teen years lifeguarding in the sun, had developed metastatic melanoma. This is a tragic irony in light of how many years I have been fighting for the passage of the sunscreen legislation.

It breaks my heart even still to write that Ellen Bernice Weisenberg died at the age of eight-one on April 18, 2016. She is survived by me, Julie Laufer of Boston, Vicki Laufer of Long Beach, Gregg Weisenberg of Long Beach and his wife, Sogdiana, Russell Weisenberg of Sarasota, Florida, and his wife, Marilyn, and six grandchildren—Brock, Max, Zachary, Daniel, Michael, and Jackie.

In a full-page article in the *Long Beach Herald,* Julie was quoted as saying about her mother and me: "She was as excited as a newlywed every time he would walk in the door. Wherever they were, they would hold hands and stop and kiss. They were stunningly affectionate with each other. Theirs was a template for their children's marriages to follow."

Ellen applied her healing talents in ways that would come to define her over the years, Julie said. She lit up the room with her glowing smile, her uncommon warmth and kindness, and those who were fortunate to know her are forever changed by these rich encounters.

Marie Curley, my former chief of staff, said: "When he was with her, she made him a more effective legislator, and her influence on him gave him more humanity and patience, and insights that he might not have seen. Along with Harvey, Ellen was a strong advocate for people with special needs or anyone who needed a champion. Ellen became a mother figure to a lot of people. She was very nurturing, and that instinct was always present in her—Ellen wanted to take care of everyone."

Barbara Tepper, a longtime friend whose husband, former Long Beach City Court Judge Roy Tepper, served on the City Council with me, said that she and Ellen shared the same philosophy of putting home and family first. "While our husbands Harvey and Roy might be front and center, we were always there as main support."

My friend Steve Kohut said that Ellen doted on our children. "She was a woman who spent her life trying to improve the world that special needs children lived in."

Everyone loved Ellen, and she loved everyone. Ellen, who always smiled, and was kind to all people, loved everyone she met. And that's the truth.

I took her ashes into the ocean after she died. A fellow lifeguard took me out in a boat. As I sat there, an old prayer that I hadn't heard since I was a boy came to me and I recited it aloud to the startled lifeguard. I was surprised I remembered every word, but I could only assume that meant God was with me. These are the words I said:

I do believe that God above
created you for me to love
He picked you out from all the rest
because He knew I love you best
I had a heart and it was true
Now it's gone from me to you
So care for it as I have done
because, my dear, you are the one
Heavenly Father up above
Please protect the one I love
Keep her always safe and sound
No matter where or when she's found
Help her to know and help her to see
That I love her, have her love me.

Just a week shy of two months after Ellen's passing in 2016, the cross street at the end of our block in Long Beach was designated "Ellen's Way," and a new street sign added for all the world to see. Just a stone's throw away, on our beautiful Long Beach Boardwalk, there's a bench with a plaque that displays the words Ellen always said: "Today is your day. . . Take in all the good life has to give." Nearby is Ricky's bench with a plaque that reads: "Dedicated to RICKY, Our Special Child, and All Special Children, for the Joy and Happiness They Bring to Our World! Ellen and Harvey Weisenberg."

More Work to Do

After Ellen died, I was invited to Albany that June to see the flowers on the Assembly desks, honoring one more time my tradition of placing flowers on everyone's desk in honor of Ellen's birthday. It was an emotional experience to be welcomed in the Assembly as a former member by the Majority Leader John J. Flanagan, who acknowledged my presence and the memory of my late wife. The Majority Leader made a presentation that alluded to the presence of the flowers over all these years, and the concept of those of us in the Assembly as being one family. He also mentioned how happy Ellen and I had been to have such a diverse and beautiful family that served the needs of people.

While in Albany, I had a press conference and rally with many of New York's largest agencies that serve people with developmental disabilities to draw attention to the need to get direct caregivers a pay raise. This was our bFair2DirectCare campaign, an effort to include $55 million in the state budget to increase wages for workers who care for the disabled.

That day speakers included representatives from the agencies, staff, parents, and residents, bringing to view the challenges that are being presented because of insufficient funding from government to be able to provide the quality care that provides a safe environment, adequate programs, and most important, staff that provide direct care to our family members. We were also fighting for a living wage, so that people who care for those with developmental disabilities do not have to work two jobs and double shifts in order to survive. It's hard to imagine, but the people hired to take care of people with disabilities are making less than fast-food workers. Further, I want to know why these workers have such a high turnover rate. People who work double shifts are tired, stressed, and in some cases, unable to provide the safe environment they are tasked with. I continue to travel throughout the state to hold news conferences and use the media to keep up my battle for worker equality.

In January 2017, I was not invited to Governor Andrew Cuomo's invitation-only State of the State address in Farmingdale. But I went anyway. I spoke to his staff and they invited me in. At some point I approached the Governor and I took his arm and said to him, "Andrew, be a hero. Give these people a living wage." He looked at me and didn't say anything, but I knew he heard me. When he presented his final budget later that month, there was no money for direct care providers. While the Governor put nothing in his budget, in my press conferences dealing with the Senate and the Assembly, and speaking to the members, we got their support. They included $55 million in their budget.

So when the Governor, the Senate, and the Assembly met to finalize the 2017 budget, we were successful in achieving getting the funding for a cost-of-living increase for workers. They were going to receive a pay raise with a schedule for increasing the state's minimum wage to $15 an hour by 2022 in six-month increments. It was a major victory. But it's not the end of the war.

Even in "retirement" I still have battles to fight. Even though I'm not in office, I make sure my voice is heard. In April 2017, I was named a winner of the week by the website *City & State New York* for my advocacy for the bFair2DirectCare campaign. I continue to travel around the state from Buffalo to eastern Long Island about this campaign. It is my mission from God to do what I can to help people who are helping others.

Conclusion

I feel as though everything I have done in my life has prepared me for my next step. My experience as a police officer led me to my drug prevention programs and to write Leandra's Law and the other vehicular crimes bills I introduced. My time as a lifeguard made me acutely aware of environmental issues, so I passed environmental bills protecting our natural resources. It also made me aware of sunscreen safety. Of course, my years as a special education teacher and as a coach made me a strong advocate for public education and reform, especially for those with special needs.

The Fight Continues

Further, as I said in the beginning of this book, my family and the place I have lived my whole life have also impacted all I have done and continue to do. Our extended family, those who are still with us, share a mutual love and respect after all the challenges we've experienced. The love that was always there when I was a child is still there today. I also feel blessed that I've lived the happiest years of my life in Long Beach. God gave us a beautiful island with thirty-five thousand people. Going through the schools from kindergarten through high school with the same friends in our small city has been like being part of a family, where everyone looked after and cared for the needs of all who lived here. I believe the diversity of our population has always been the strength of our community. It's interesting to this day, more than eighty years later, even though the city continues to change, that there's still the feeling of love and respect for all who reside here.

I continue to advocate for Long Beach. I still maintain as I did back when I was on the City Council that Long Beach is recreation with the beautiful resources we have. People continue to come here to enjoy our ocean and beach. As such, instead of the current focus on building more high-rise developments, I would like to see the people who reside here have access to more recreation, like music and art. I think there should also be a focus on the needs of the infrastructure of our community and trying to maintain a living tax rate so that the diversity of our population can continue.

Regarding my work in the Assembly, I believe my biggest accomplishment is my commitment to be the voice to those who have no voice. Helping to restore $145 million to New York's developmentally disabled has been a significant achievement for me.

I continue to stand for the same causes that propelled me for my entire career: Tough enforcement and punishment of crime, but strong gun control; strong government to help those in need, especially the disabled; Republican issues like tough DWI laws and reverence for the American flag; Democratic issues like abortion rights, gay marriage, and tolerance; low taxes, but strong spending for schools, first responders, and infrastructure. My core principles are: Protecting the rights and dignity of our most vulnerable citizens; loyalty to community, state, and nation; protecting the public from crime; protecting the public from danger, like predators, drunk driving, dangerous products, and environmental damage; balanced budgets, honest government, and transparency in politics. That's why I keep showing up when asked—and even when I'm not—to fight for what matters.

But there are other common-sense bills I have proposed that have still not been signed, though in one case I have been trying since 2001. Being aware that a person dies every hour from melanoma, skin cancer, I passed legislation for twenty years, sometimes unanimously in the Assembly, two-hundred-thirteen members statewide. It would require sunscreens to carry a "best-if-used by" date. Professional campaigns by the American Cancer Society and American Association of Pediatrics have planted the seeds about greater sun protection. The Cancer Society of New York and all cancer agencies have supported this legislation. The Senate would not pass this legislation because of the influence of lobbyists from Estee Lauder. It finally did in June 2014. But Governor

Andrew Cuomo vetoed this bill in December 2014. He still does not support this legislation that would help prevent skin cancer. The truth is that government can do great good and ultimately, the truth will prevail.

Something else that upsets me is that earlier this year, a man who was convicted of murdering two police officers, was released on parole. Herman Bell was convicted in 1979 of the 1971 murders of Police Officers Joseph Piagentini and Waverly Jones in Harlem. He was also convicted of the 1971 murder of a California cop. He served nearly 40 years behind bars before he was released.. I wrote about the death penalty bill I advocated for back in 1989, saying I was in favor of it for criminals who murder peace, police, or corrections officers. Mario Cuomo vetoed it every year. And now, in 2018, someone who should never see freedom again is out of jail. I'm sure there is no other state that would offer parole to a man who killed police officers. Instead, this man should have served life without parole. Is this justice in New York?

Meanwhile, I have other causes and missions I continue to support. In July 2017, *Surf for All* had been around for five years. The Long Beach-based nonprofit organization continues to organize surf outings and events for veterans, disadvantaged youth, and people with a range of physical and developmental disabilities. That summer, we launched a new adaptive surf camp at New York Beach Club in Atlantic Beach. It was the first of its kind in New York. It's tuition-free and sponsored by the Harvey & Ellen Weisenberg Foundation. It provides a full camp experience for the young athletes, with a week of surf lessons to help foster skill development, as well as adaptive educational, art, and communication units designed by a staff of teachers, school psychologists, and administrators. We have a range of adaptive equipment, like jet-powered surfboards, special life vests, and sand-traversing wheelchairs.

It gives me great joy to get out there in the water with the campers. I worked four weeks, four hours a day, four days a week as a lifeguard. I thought I was going to change and enhance the lives of these people, when in fact they changed and enhanced my life. At the end of the summer, I took all the volunteers and staff out to dinner. Being a professional lifeguard, I told them I would have to be paid—the salary of one dollar. At dinner that night, they presented me with a check for one dollar, which I have framed. I had also donated $5,000 to the program. I'll be working there again this summer.

After Hurricane Harvey in October 2017, I wanted to reclaim my name, so through the Harvey & Ellen Weisenberg Foundation, I donated $10,000 to a Houston facility for people with special needs. I reached out to my bank, the Bethpage Federal Credit Union, which was fundraising money for hurricane victims. They in turn reached out to the United Way of Long Island, whose Houston counterpart suggested I send my check to The Center, which provides a wide range of services. My check was matched by a couple from the Houston area for a total of $40,000.

In April 2017, I served as the grand marshal for the 2017 Long Island Autism Walk and Resource Fair.

In November 2017, Governor Andrew Cuomo invited me to Albany for the announcement of a $354 million resiliency project to improve the water quality of Long Island's Western Bays, which we had begun in 2010.

In December 2017, I led a rally in Albany to call on legislators to speed up the already approved wage increases because 2022 is too long to wait for a fair wage. I said that some caregivers, mostly women and people of color, are so poorly paid they have been choosing to work in the fast-food industry instead, and that low salaries create high turnover rates and staffing shortages at many care facilities throughout the state. There has been a fourteen percent reduction in staff of direct care givers statewide. Also, statistics have indicated that in the first six months, one-third of all new people leave. A half a million people are impacted by what is taking place.

I received a letter earlier this year, 2018, from bFair2DirectCare thanking me for my help. They called me a champion, a hero, a superstar, and a mensch. It was signed by the Alliance of Long Island Agencies, Cerebral Palsy Associations of New York State, The Developmental Disability Alliance of Western New York, Direct Support Professional Alliance of New York State, The InterAgency Council of Developmental Disabilities Agencies, The NYS Association of Community and Residential Agencies, New York State Rehabilitation Association, and Self-Advocacy Association of New York State.

I also continue to make donations in the name of the Harvey & Ellen Weisenberg Foundation. This year I established a $25,000 endowment scholarship in Ricky's name, the Ricky Weisenberg Endowed Scholarship. Ours is the only one for people with disabilities, and it's forever. It will be awarded to a qualified student with a demonstrated disability or special needs, and will be selected on the basis of academic achievement and/or financial need. I chose Hofstra because it's where I earned my Master of Science degree in education in 1962 to begin my teaching career in special education and was awarded my honorary doctorate.

This year I also established a $25,000 endowment scholarship in Ellen's name recognizing her career as a nurse. The Ellen Weisenberg Endowed Scholarship will provide one student annually in the Stony Brook School of Nursing, Nurse Practitioner Program to receive more advanced education regarding treatment of patients with disabilities at a clinically-based program at Long Island Select Healthcare. As part of this program, the nurse practitioners also have the opportunity to provide direct care to individuals with developmental and physical disabilities.

It makes me happy to know that both of these scholarships in the names of two people I love dearly will help make a difference.

Further, each year since 2011 I have given away my pension to agencies that take care of our special children for a total so far of nearly $400,000. It's something Ellen and I felt would be a good way to thank and support these agencies in the work that they do. Among those I gave to are in order of donations made: Hebrew University; United Cerebral Palsy—Nassau County; AHRC Foundation—Nassau County; Long Beach Lions Club; Nassau County Firefighters Pipes and Drums; Nassau County Police PBA; Long Beach Reach School; Long Beach MLK; Camp Sunrise; Stony Brook Hospital Child Center Foundation; JCC Friedberg Pre-K; Plainview Hospital (special children care); Hofstra University George Estabrook Alumni Association; South Nassau Communities Hospital; Ronald McDonald House; New York City PBA for widows and children; Holocaust Memorial Committee of Long Island; Inwood Fire Department Joseph Sanford Jr. Fund; Israel National LAX; Long Beach Fire Department; Nassau County Detectives; Syosset Hospital; Make-a-Wish Foundation; the Harvey & Ellen Weisenberg Foundation Special Needs Resources Corp; AARP Foundation; Christian Light Missionary Baptist Church; and Long Beach High School.

I am also frequently asked to speak at events. Since January of this year, I have been a keynote speaker at Boricua College in Brooklyn, Nassau Community College, Pace University, Hunter School of Social Work, and Hofstra, as well as a statewide speaker for AHRC and UPC. I'm always asked to speak to parents, families, faculty, and staff about special needs issues.

I keep myself busy. Just this past weekend I spent my Saturday morning on Long Beach in the ocean helping an athlete to surf. She was from the Challenged Athletes Foundation, based in San Diego, which provides physically challenged people with the tools they need to pursue active and healthy lifestyles. Then I went to the lifeguard certification for two hours in my role as the Lifeguard Examiner.

Sunday morning I spent two hours teaching a safety lifesaving course for eight- to eleven-year-olds, many of whom are the grandchildren of people I coached years ago. I also sponsor the Long Beach-based Artists in Partnership organization in their therapeutic intergenerational movement and socialization workshops. In this program, high school students in special education and senior citizens from the Magnolia Senior Center enjoy a dance program together. I also sponsor a chair yoga program at the Long Beach Library for senior citizens. I made a visit there one winter day when it was snowing and the room was still full. And I still do *Surf for All* every summer.

But always there is still Ricky to care for. I visit my now sixty-year-old son at AHRC in Plainview. My goal is always to give him a happy day and show him how much he is loved. I bring him his favorite cheesecake, hot tea, and graham crackers, exactly as Ellen and I have been doing every week for decades. These days Vicki comes with me and we spend time together, the three of us. Ricky responds with his smile. He takes comfort from a rattle-like toy that Ellen made for him long ago; she made several so he always has one.

Ricky is my angel, Ellen was a saint, and together, they gave my life a mission. My advice to families of special needs children is to remember that there is nothing greater or more virtuous than being a giver, and to relish the small signs of love from your special children—the greatest return on investment that can ever be had.

I keep this handwritten note from another father of a special needs son, a young man who did not get to grow older, as a reminder of all the work I have done, and whatever I can still do as long as I'm able:

I thank God for Harvey. He is a champion for children and adults with disabilities. If it were not for Harvey, numerous key laws to protect our most vulnerable would not be in place today. Harvey sponsored Jonathan's Law, which gives families access to abuse and neglect investigation records that were previously concealed from them. My wife Lisa and I approached Harvey because of his son Ricky who has special needs knowing that he would readily help change this gross injustice.

—Signed, Michael Carey, the proud father of Jonathan Carey, who had autism and was only thirteen when he was killed by his caregivers.

As I look back on the public work I have done, it's clear that so much has been as the result of ordinary citizens like the Careys who took on causes that initially seemed hopeless, but eventually changed the country. I learned first-hand that democracy involves messy power struggles between competing interests. The good guys don't always win. Even when they do win, it's usually after they lose several rounds first. But dedicated citizens and good politicians often succeed and should not throw in the towel. If we give up on government, we give up on ourselves.

I believe that government, citizens, and politicians can rise above their narrow interests and get things done. Fighting for the public good and for your community is the most rewarding vocation a person can have. As a result, I have more friends than I can count in my own community and around the country. I have been blessed in my life.

I believe the pessimists and cynics are wrong. Government is not the enemy, and it sometimes does a world of good. Politicians aren't angels, but plenty of them—more than you might think in this current political climate—fight hard to make their communities a better place. If we give up on politics and government, we give up on ourselves. We create a self-fulfilling prophecy. If you believe your elected leaders are cynical and purely self-interested, they will probably be as bad as you expect. If everybody acts as though the system is rigged, no one with any self-respect will want to run for office. We'll be left with political hacks who don't give a damn about the public interest, basically seeking office for power and money.

Local politics are a mirror for all politics. Politics are about people, and people are at their most real in their own communities. That's true for the best and the worst that people have to offer. For all the chicanery and frustrations I experienced in my thirty-eight years in politics, I'm still amazed at the genuine good accomplished by hard-working and dedicated activists and political leaders who fight long and hard for what is right. I am still proud to have been a member of an institution that successfully does so much for so many.